CAMBRIDGE LIBRARY COLLECTION

Books of enduring scholarly value

Travel and Exploration

The history of travel writing dates back to the Bible, Caesar, the Vikings and the Crusaders, and its many themes include war, trade, science and recreation. Explorers from Columbus to Cook charted lands not previously visited by Western travellers, and were followed by merchants, missionaries, and colonists, who wrote accounts of their experiences. The development of steam power in the nineteenth century provided opportunities for increasing numbers of 'ordinary' people to travel further, more economically, and more safely, and resulted in great enthusiasm for travel writing among the reading public. Works included in this series range from first-hand descriptions of previously unrecorded places, to literary accounts of the strange habits of foreigners, to examples of the burgeoning numbers of guidebooks produced to satisfy the needs of a new kind of traveller - the tourist.

Sketches of Persia

Sketches of Persia, although published anonymously in 1827, is attributed to Sir John Malcolm (1769–1833). Malcolm was a diplomat and administrator in India: arriving at the age of fourteen in 1783 to work for the East India Company, he was known during his long career as 'Boy' Malcolm. He swiftly moved into more political and diplomatic roles. He became fluent in Persian and was despatched to Persia for part of his career, though he would eventually return to India and become Governor of Bombay (1827–1830). In Volume 1 of *Sketches*, Malcolm starts the journey from Bombay, sailing into the Persian Gulf, arriving at Abusheher, where he stays many weeks. From there his party moves inland into the mountains, and finally reaches Shiraz and then Persepolis. Throughout his journey, Malcolm fills this work with his observations about the people he meets, and recounts Persian folk stories and fables.

T0382211

Cambridge University Press has long been a pioneer in the reissuing of out-of-print titles from its own backlist, producing digital reprints of books that are still sought after by scholars and students but could not be reprinted economically using traditional technology. The Cambridge Library Collection extends this activity to a wider range of books which are still of importance to researchers and professionals, either for the source material they contain, or as landmarks in the history of their academic discipline.

Drawing from the world-renowned collections in the Cambridge University Library, and guided by the advice of experts in each subject area, Cambridge University Press is using state-of-the-art scanning machines in its own Printing House to capture the content of each book selected for inclusion. The files are processed to give a consistently clear, crisp image, and the books finished to the high quality standard for which the Press is recognised around the world. The latest print-on-demand technology ensures that the books will remain available indefinitely, and that orders for single or multiple copies can quickly be supplied.

The Cambridge Library Collection will bring back to life books of enduring scholarly value (including out-of-copyright works originally issued by other publishers) across a wide range of disciplines in the humanities and social sciences and in science and technology.

Sketches of Persia

From the Journals of a Traveller in the East

VOLUME 1

JOHN MALCOLM

CAMBRIDGE UNIVERSITY PRESS

Cambridge, New York, Melbourne, Madrid, Cape Town,
Singapore, São Paolo, Delhi, Tokyo, Mexico City

Published in the United States of America by Cambridge University Press, New York

www.cambridge.org
Information on this title: www.cambridge.org/9781108028660

© in this compilation Cambridge University Press 2011

This edition first published 1827
This digitally printed version 2011

ISBN 978-1-108-02866-0 Paperback

This book reproduces the text of the original edition. The content and language reflect
the beliefs, practices and terminology of their time, and have not been updated.

Cambridge University Press wishes to make clear that the book, unless originally published
by Cambridge, is not being republished by, in association or collaboration with, or
with the endorsement or approval of, the original publisher or its successors in title.

SKETCHES

OF

PERSIA,

FROM THE

JOURNALS OF A TRAVELLER IN THE EAST.

IN TWO VOLUMES.

VOL. I.

LONDON:

JOHN MURRAY, ALBEMARLE-STREET.

MDCCCXXVII.

LONDON:

PRINTED BY THOMAS DAVISON, WHITEFRIARS.

THESE VOLUMES

ARE INSCRIBED

TO

JOHN FLEMING, Esq., M.D., F.R.S., &c.

LATE PRESIDENT OF THE MEDICAL BOARD OF CALCUTTA,

BY

HIS MOST SINCERE AND ATTACHED FRIEND,

THE TRAVELLER.

INTRODUCTION.

ONCE upon a time this Island of Great Britain had some spots where men and women and little children dwelt, or were believed to dwell, in innocence, ignorance, and content. Travellers seldom visited them; poets saw them in their dreams, and novelists told stories of them; but these days are now past. Thanks to steam-boats and stage-coaches, there is not a spot to which an ignorant or sage human being can retire, where his eye will not be delighted or offended by a dark column of smoke, or his ear gratified or grated by the rattling wheels of a carriage. It is perhaps a consequence of this invasion of retirement that all are tempted from their

homes, and that while one half of the population is on the highways the other half is
on the narrow seas. This love of travel,
however, is in the vast majority limited to
the neighbouring countries of Europe; but
the ardour of curiosity, and an ambitious desire of escaping from the beaten track, has
of late years induced not a few scientific
and enterprising travellers to overrun the
renowned lands of Greece and Egypt, whose
inhabitants stare with astonishment at men
flying with impatience from town to town,
exploring ruins; measuring pyramids; grop-
ing in dark caverns; analyzing the various
properties of earth, air, and water; carrying
off mutilated gods and goddesses; packing
up common stones and pebbles, as if they
were rubies and diamonds; and even bearing
away the carcases of the dead, strangely
preferring the withered frame of a female

mummy, which has been mouldering for four thousand years in its sepulchre, to the loveliest specimens of living and animated beauty.

The uninformed natives of these countries, whose condition is much to be deplored, are not aware that the great Samuel Johnson has said, that " Whatever raises the past, the distant, and the future, above the present, exalts us in the dignity of human beings;" which is an unanswerably good reason for the preference given to mummies over every living object, however fascinating.

The rage of the present day for mummies and other delectable reliques of antiquity has deluged Egypt with itinerant men of science and research, who have quite exhausted that land of wonders; and those who have lately visited it have been reduced, from actual want of other aliment, to the necessity of preying upon their predecessors, many of whom have been cruelly mangled, and some wholly devoured.

These wandering tribes of writers, who are, in a certain degree, subject to the same motives which force the hordes of Tartary to change their places of abode, have recently begun to migrate into Syria, Asia Minor, and some have actually penetrated as far as Persia. This has given me no small alarm, for I have long had designs upon that country myself: I had seen something of it, and had indulged a hope that I might, at my leisure, gratify the public by allowing them to participate in my stock of information ; but being of an indolent disposition I deferred the execution of this, my favourite plan, until that anticipated period of repose, the prospect of which, however distant, has always cheered a life of vicissitude and labour.

Nothing that had hitherto appeared respecting Persia at all frightened me. I am no historian, therefore I did not tremble at Sir John Malcolm's ponderous quartos; I am no tourist, Mr. Morier's Journeys gave me no uneasiness; the learned Researches of Sir William Ouseley were enough to terrify an antiquarian, but that was not my trade; and, as I happen to have clumsy, untaught fingers, and little if any taste for the picturesque, I viewed, without alarm, the splendid volumes of Sir Robert Ker Porter. Far different, however, was the case when that rogue Hajji Baba made his appearance. I perused him with anxiety, but was consoled by finding that, though he approached the very borders of my province, he had made no serious inroads. I was roused, however, into action, and determined instantly to rum-

mage those trunks into which my sketches
had been thrown as they were finished, and
where many of them had slumbered undis-
turbed for nearly thirty years.

I must warn the reader that the trunks
here spoken of bear no resemblance whatever to those imaginary boxes which it has
lately been the fashion to discover, filled with
MSS., unaccountably deposited in them by
some strange and mysterious wight; mine
are all real, well-made, strong, iron-clamped
boxes, which I had prepared with great care,
in order that they might preserve the papers
I from time to time intrusted to them   I
am well aware that this plain and true state-
ment of the fact will, with many, diminish
the interest of these pages; but with others
it will increase it; for they will be gratified
to find in them sketches taken on the spot,

while the facts and the feelings to which they relate were fresh and warm before me ; and I can truly affirm, that the sense, the nonsense, the anecdotes, the fables, and the tales,—all, in short, which these volumes contain, with the exception of a few sage reflections of my own, do actually belong to the good people amongst whom they profess to have been collected.

Yet partial as I was to my secret hoard, it was long before I could make up my mind to publish. While I was one day musing upon the subject, my attention was accidentally drawn to a volume of Persian poetry that was lying on the table. A fâl or lot, I exclaimed, shall put an end to my indecision ! Saying which, according to the usage of my Persian friends in like cases, I shut my eyes, opened the book, and counting seven pages back, read the first four lines, as follows :

" Her kih sefer kerdeh pesendeedeh sheved
Z'àeena-e-noor kemâl-esh deedeh sheved
Pâkeezeter ez âb nebâshed cheezee
Her jâh kih kooned mekâm gendeedeh sheved."

" Whoever has travelled shall be approved ;
His perfections shall be reflected as from a mirror
of light.
There can be nothing more pure than water ;
But wherever it stagnates it becomes offensive."

My delight was excessive, and I despatched
my manuscripts forthwith to the bookseller ;
who has been desired to keep me minutely
informed of the success of these volumes ;
and a hint has been given him, that if they
meet with encouragement, the contents of
the boxes before mentioned are far from
being exhausted.

NOTE TO THE READER.

The usual orthography of some proper names has been altered, with a view of rendering them more conformable to the pronunciation and the grammar of the languages to which they belong. For instance, our old friend and favourite, the caliph Haroun-al-Raschid of the Arabian Tales, appears under his Arabic name of Haroon-oor-Rasheed. The critical reader will also discover that a few of the eastern words have not always been spelled exactly alike. This unintentional typographical inaccuracy was caused by the peculiar circumstances under which these volumes were printed.

CONTENTS

OF

VOL. I.

SKETCHES OF PERSIA.

CHAPTER I.

VOYAGE FROM BOMBAY TO THE PERSIAN GULF.

THERE is a monotony in a long sea-voyage,
particularly to passengers, which those who have
never traversed the wide ocean cannot well understand. A fair or contrary wind, a calm or a
storm, a man overboard, a strange sail, or the hook-
ing of a shark, are events which rouse for the moment; but the passenger soon sinks again into his
listless, restless life, sitting half an hour below,
walking another half hour on deck, holding on by
the rigging when the ship rolls, looking over the
gangway when the sea is smooth, watching the
man casting the log, and waiting with anxiety to
hear the latitude announced at twelve o'clock. His
little incidents are, being in the way of the officer

of the watch when upon deck, and when below
disturbing the captain's calculations of the longi-
tude, by laughing or talking with other idlers; for
that is the class in which he is registered in the
muster-roll of the crew. With me, however, there
is a pursuit which helps to beguile a long voyage.
I am always on the look-out for odd characters,
and these abound at sea; from which circumstance,
I suppose, we have our common phrase of calling
an out-of-the-way person " an odd fish," alluding to
the element where he is generally found. Such a
one I met on board the frigate in which we sailed
for Persia, and I shall give a sketch of him as taken
at the moment.

This man, whose name was Peterson, was what
he appeared to be, a blunt sailor : his experience
in the Indian seas recommended him to the situation he now occupied, as acting master of a frigate :
he was a figure to play Falstaff, being very stout,
and nearly six feet high. He wore his clothes
loose, and, when he came on board, a sailor, struck
with his appearance, turning his quid as he eyed
him, exclaimed " We shall never be in distress for
canvas; our new master wears a spare set of sails."

I shall give Peterson's history in his own words, as related after dinner the day he came on board. " I have been," said he, " thirty-two years at sea, and have seen both calms and storms. When a young man, I was stuck full of arrows by some savage Americans; and but for a tobacco-box, which stopped one that hit upon a vital part, I should have gone to Davy's locker at that time. Since I came to this country, twenty-eight years ago, I have had many ups and downs, but weathered them all pretty tolerably till three years since, when coming to Bombay in a small sloop, I was laid on board by some pirates belonging to Bate *. We fought as well as we could, but the rascals were too many for us, and while we were defending one part of the vessel they sprung on board at another, giving a fire at the same time, which killed my owner close beside me. A passenger then jumped overboard, for which, thought I, ' you are a fool ;' for let the worst come to the worst, a man may do that at any time. One of these fellows looking at me cried ' Mar hara-mee,' which means, ' kill the rascal.' ' Mut

* The island of Bate is situated at the north-western extremity of the Gulf of Cutch.

mar,' ' don't kill him,' said a soft-hearted looking
fellow, and defended me from the blow; so they
did not kill me, but stripped and bound me to the
capstan, and away they took us to Bate. When
we came there, the chief or head fellow came on
board, and I fully expected we should be sent
ashore and hanged. When this chap sent for me,
I was a pretty figure; I had not been shaved for
three weeks, and I was wrapped round with a top-
gallant studding sail. ' What are you?' said the
fellow. ' An Englishman,' said I. ' Very well; I
won't kill you.' ' Faith,' thinks I, ' I'm very glad of
that.' ' My people,' says he, ' are all big thieves.'
' Egad,' thinks I, ' you are the biggest of the gang.'
He then asked me what money or property I had;
and I thought at one time he looked as if he would
have given it back; so I tells him all, even to my
gold watch. The whole was about five thousand
rupees. ' Well, well,' says he, ' it shall be taken
care of;' and I suppose it was, for I never saw a
rap of it, only five rupees that the villain gave me,
in a present, as he called it, to bear my expenses
when he sent me and my crew to Bombay.

" I left Bate, notwithstanding my losses, as happy

as could be, to get out of their clutches alive; and
after some days we reached Bombay in a pretty
pickle; my feet were swelled, I had not shaved
since my capture, and I had only a few ragged
clothes on. Two rupees were left out of the five,
and with them I went to a tavern and ordered
breakfast; when it was over I told one of the servants to call his master. In came an English
waiter, with his head all powdered, shuffling and
mincing, saying, as he entered the room, ' Do you
want me, sir?'   ' Yes,' says I, ' I want you:
I have been plundered, and have got no cash, and
will thank you to lend me twenty or thirty rupees.'
' What are you—a common sailor?'   ' Not quite,'
says I ; ' but I want the money to get a few clothes,
and then I can go to my friends.'   ' I am not master
of this house,' said this gentleman, and out he skips.
I saw no more of him or his twenty rupees; and
when I told a servant to get me a tiffin, he said, I
had not paid for my breakfast. As I was jawing
with this fellow, a Parsee* came in, and asked me if

* Parsee is the name of the descendants of the ancient Persians,
who still retain the usages and religion of their forefathers. There
are many of these followers of Zoroaster at Bombay, where they

I had not better go to the bazar, and borrow some
clothes, and then go to my friends. Well, God
knows, I had not much heart to do any thing; for
the unkindness of my countryman, after all I had ṣuf-
fered, cut me just as if I had been cut with á knife;
but I thought I might as well follow the Parsee,
who was one of those fellows that go about Bombay
trying what they can make of every body they meet.
I goes first to one shop, and tries things on; and
when they fit, I says, ' I will pay you to-morrow;'
but the fellow says, ' No; ready money.' Well,
I was obliged to strip again: this happened at four
shops, and I was quite tired, when a good fellow,
who keeps No. 18, of the Great Bazar, said, I
might fit myself, and pay when I could. I then
got rigged, and stood away for Mr. Adamson,
whom I had before known. I met him at the door
of his house, and he did not know me; but when
I told him my story—' Oh !' says he, quite pitiful,
' are you the poor fellow who has suffered so much ?
I will get you a birth in another ship—and take
this.' So saying, he gives me one hundred rupees.

form, if not the most numerous, the most respectable part of the
native community.

Well, I thanked him; and next goes to Captain Phillips, and got from him a present of two gold mohurs, and six suits of good clothes, from top to toe. He made me report and write three or four sheets about Bate, and how I had been used; and then sent me to the governor, Mr. Duncan, who gets all the long story from me again, and then gave me one hundred rupees. I had now two hundred and thirty rupees and clean rigging. I goes again to the tavern, and sings out lustily for tiffin. Well, they look and sees I am quite a different thing from before, and so become mighty civil and attentive. The waiter begs my pardon— says he was mistaken—and that he had twenty rupees ready, and would give me any aid I liked. ' D—n your aid,' says I; ' you are very ready to give it to any person who does not want it.' It was a great treat to me to serve him as I did: I eat my tiffin, paid for it on the table, and left the house.

" Well," said Peterson, " to make a long story short, I went in a China ship, and, last year, got the command of a vessel belonging to a Persian merchant, who trades to the Gulf. He was a bad

owner, had no credit, and, what with that and the
fear of the Arabs, I had a troublesome time of it.
We parted; and he has got another captain, rather
black to be sure, but he likes him all the better, I
suppose, from being nearer his own vile colour
than I was; and I, by this means, being along
shore, having no money or credit, am glad to come
as acting-master of this here ship. I thank God
I have good health, and don't complain; many are
worse off than I am."

Such was our Master's * history. In a conversation I had with him, as we were walking the
deck, the day we arrived at Muscat, I asked him
if he had a wife? " No;" said he. " You were
never married, then?" " I didn't say so," he replied. " I beg your pardon," said I. " Oh! no
harm, no harm! the honest truth never need be
hid: I was married; but taking a long voyage,
being away seven years, and my letters (of which,
by the by, I wrote but few) miscarrying, what
does my wife do, but marries again. This I heard

* This old sailor is now no more. He continued unlucky till he
found a generous patron at Bombay, whose active benevolence gave
repose and comfort to his latter days.

when I got home to England." " And what did you do ?" said I ; " did you inquire after her ?" " Indeed I did not," said Peterson with great indifference; " I didn't think her worth so much trouble ; she was glad, I suppose, to get rid of me, and, God knows, I was not sorry to be shot of her."

The vicissitudes to which sailors are subject train them to bear what are termed the ups and downs of life better than any other men in the world. They appear, when afloat, not only to leave all their cares on shore, but to forget the hardships incident to their condition. A remarkable instance of this was given by our captain, who told us, that he went one day to see a tender, on board which there was a great number of men who had just been pressed, and who, though strictly confined in their floating prison, were, nevertheless, joining in the chorus of one of our patriotic airs, and singing with great glee the old song—

" Who are so free as we sons of the waves ?"

CHAPTER II.

" LAND from the mast-head !"   " What does it
look like ?"   " High land, sir, on the larboard bow,
stretching away to the north-west."   " Can you see
land to starboard ?"   " No."   " Then," says the
captain, with some little swell, " we have just hit
it ; the watch is a good one ; and three or four
hours of this will bring us into Muscat." The pre-
diction proved correct.   Now, if I understood per-
spective and retrospective, how I would delight my
readers by contrasting the barren rocky hills of
Arabia, where not a trace of vegetable nature is to
be found, with the shaded shores of Ceylon, and
the dark forests that clothe the lofty mountains of
Malabar ! But I am not a picturesque traveller ;
suffice it therefore to say, the arid hills we were
now contemplating protect, by almost encircling it,
a cove, at the extremity of which is a small plain,
crowded with high houses, which form the city of
Muscat. This emporium to the trade of the Persian Gulf is defended by batteries, which command
its narrow entrance, as well as by fortifications that

cover every part of the uneven and mis-shapen hills and crags around it.

Muscat is governed by a prince whose title is Imam, and whose authority, like that of many chiefs in Arabia, is more of a patriarchal than despotic character. Though he has large fleets, including some fine frigates, and a considerable army to garrison his possessions on the coast of Africa, the shores of Arabia, and the islands of the Persian Gulf, he must attend to the summons of any inhabitant of Muscat who calls him to a court of justice. Your sceptics who deny the existence of any just admininistration of power, except in the commonwealth of Europe, may call this a mere form. Be it so: yet the knowledge that such a form was observed went far, in my mind, to mark the character of this petty government. But it is the eye, the disposition, and the judgment of the observer, more than what is actually seen, that stamps the condition of distant nations with those who have to form their opinions at second-hand; and the generality of readers, who have their happiness grounded on a natural prejudice in favour of their own ways and usages, lean toward such as minister to their pride and patriotism, by throwing

a dark shade on all they meet different from old
England, or some of those countries in its vicinity,
for which their good climate, cheap viands, and well
flavoured wines, have created a predilection.

The eastern hemisphere continues to have a certain venerable air with old men from a belief that
the star of knowledge first enlightened its horizon :
children delight in it from its containing the enchanting tales of the " Thousand and one Nights;"
ladies admire its flowered muslins, rich shawls, pure
pearls, and brilliant diamonds ; merchants view it
as a source of commercial wealth ; the naturalist,
the botanist, and the geologist, search its plains, its
forests, and its mountains, for unicorns, spikenard,
splendid specimens of zeolite, and grand basaltic
formations ; the English soldier looks to its fields
for a harvest of reputation ; while pious missionaries
sally forth with more than military zeal, to reclaim
the millions of the East from their errors, and direct
them in the path of life.

Almost all these, however different their objects,
concur in one sentiment, that the rulers of the East
are despots, and their subjects slaves ; that the former are cruel, the latter degraded and miserable,
and both equally ignorant.

I had seen the father of the present Imam of
Muscat when I accompanied a former mission to
Persia; we had been introduced to him on board
the Ganjava, his flag ship, of a thousand tons bur-
then, and carrying forty guns. We found him,
though surrounded with some state, very simply
attired; he had a shawl rolled round his head as a
turban, and the Arab cloak, which hung over his
plain robes, was of white broad-cloth, no way ornamented; he wore no jewels, and had no arms, not
even a dagger, about his person: his manner was
plain and manly, and marked his active enterprising
character. The eyes of his crew (Arabs, Nubians,
and Abyssinians), who were upon or near the quarter-
deck, though they wandered now and then among
his visitors, were usually fixed on their prince; but
their countenances indicated affection, not fear; and
I could not but observe that he never looked at or
spoke to any of them but with kindness.

During this visit, while we were sitting under
the awning spread over the deck, several captains
of his largest vessels, who had just arrived from
Bussorah, came on board. The Imam was in the
cabin with the Envoy, and, before he came out, I
was pleased to see the hearty manner in which these

commanders saluted and were received by almost all
on board. " Salâm alicum!" (peace be with you!)
was heard from all, while every one who met a
friend took his right hand, and, after shaking it,
raised it as high as his breast. What appeared singular, was the extent of this cordial and familiar
greeting; it was not limited by those rules which
are found necessary in more civilised societies. The
Arab sailor, however low his occupation, exhibited
an ease and independence in addressing the commanders, which showed that, as far as the intercourse between man and man was concerned, he
deemed himself his equal. I asked a person sitting
near me, if this familiarity did not now and then
interfere with discipline? " No," he answered;
" the line is well undertood, and in cases of devia-
tion there is a severe punishment; for with us
Arabs the right of addressing our superiors, as you
have now seen, is our proudest privilege, and its
loss, which would be the consequence of the abuse
of it, would be deeply felt, both as a privation and
a disgrace."

The above scene was interrupted by the opening
of the cabin door, and every one fell into his place
as the Imam came upon deck. He stood while the

commanders, who had returned from their voyage, advanced in their turns, according to their rank, and, taking his extended right hand in both theirs, pressed it, at the same time bending their bodies in a low bow, after which they raised their right hand in salutation to their head, then placing it on their heart, retired backwards. The Imam, after this ceremony was ended, seated himself, desiring us and all his principal officers to do the same.

We had a dinner prepared on board, of which the whole party partook; and when we came away, I was struck, as we passed under-the stern of the vessel, by seeing some of the Imam's ladies, among whom was his favourite wife, unveiled, looking at us with eager curiosity. They appeared much pleased, which we imputed to the notice the Envoy had taken of the Imam's sons, two fine boys, each of whom was gratified with appropriate presents.

The view I had taken of the Imam's court—the intercourse we had with him, his sons, and chief officers—the security which I observed merchants and other inhabitants, both Mahomedan and Hindu, enjoying at Muscat, gave me a very pleasing impression of that place, and I had made a sketch of the manners and customs of the people, no way unfavourable. This I showed one day to a friend, who was a captain in the navy, who, rather to my surprise, burst into a fit of laughter, and said, he could show me a very opposite picture of the same scene. " There is an order from the Admiralty," said he, " that the officers of a man-of-war, when they visit a port little known, should describe the manners and customs of the inhabitants. I have a blunt fellow of a master, an excellent seaman, but who troubles himself very little with matters on shore. Curious to have his observations, and knowing that he had two or three times visited the town of Muscat, I insisted on his complying with orders, and filling up the column of his journal. He evaded this duty as long as he could : at last, in despair, he went to his cabin, and returning with his book, said ' There, sir, I have obeyed orders, and you will find all I could write about these black fellows, and all they deserve.' I took the journal and read,

' Inhabitants of Muscat.

' As to manners, they have none; and their customs are very beastly.' "

This picture of the good master will no doubt be deemed by many truer than mine; and travellers who limit their observations to the busy beach, crowded with slaves, covered with packages of dates, blackened with flies, and scented with putrid salt fish, will be certain to prefer this laconic description of this rude and dirty people; or supposing them to enter the vile narrow streets of the town, and see (as they may) strings of slaves walking, with a man following and calling out their prices as he exhibits them in this ambulatory auction. "Number one—handsome young man, five hundred piastres; number two—a little older, but very healthy and strong, four hundred piastres;" and so on till he describes his whole string of unhappy bipeds. Who would not turn with indignation and disgust from such filth and abomination!

If, however, we have nerve enough to look a little farther into the scene which has been described, we shall find that the reason why houses are crowded upon each other, till cleanliness becomes impossible, is because men and their property are protected at this port against injustice and oppression; and our disgust at the effect will in a great degree be removed by contemplating the cause. Even with regard to the sale of slaves, of which Muscat

is the great mart, though the mode of disposing of
them appears to justify the master's designation of
the inhabitants as " beastly in their customs," yet
when we take a comparative view of the fate of the
victims of this commerce, from the stain of which
our own country is hardly yet purified, and which
is still carried on, openly or clandestinely, by almost
every power of civilised Europe, we shall be compelled to acknowledge the superior humanity of
Asiatic nations.

The slave in eastern countries, after he is trained
to service, attains the condition of a favoured domestic; his adoption of the religion of his master is
usually the first step which conciliates the latter.
Except at a few sea-ports, he is seldom put to hard
labour.   In Asia there are no fields tilled by slaves,
no manufactories in which they are doomed to toil;
their occupations are all of a domestic nature, and
good behaviour is rewarded by kindness and confidence, which raises them in the community to
which they belong.   The term gholam, or slave, in
Mahomedan countries, is not one of opprobrium,
nor does it even convey the idea of a degraded
condition.   The Georgians, Nubians, and Abys-

sinians, and even the Seedee, or Caffree, as the woolly-headed Africans are called, are usually married, and their children, who are termed house-born*, become, in a manner, part of their master's family. They are deemed the most attached of his adherents : they often inherit a considerable portion of his wealth ; and not unfrequently (with the exception of the woolly-headed Caffree) lose, by a marriage in his family, or by some other equally respectable connexion, all trace of their origin.

According to the Mahomedan law, the state of slavery is divided into two conditions—the perfect and absolute, or imperfect and privileged. Those who belong to the first class are, with all their property, at the disposal of their masters. The second, though they cannot, before emancipation, inherit or acquire property, have many privileges, and cannot be sold or transferred. A female, who has a child to her master, belongs to the privileged class ; as does a slave, to whom his master has promised his liberty, on the payment of a certain sum, or on his death.

The greatest encouragement is given in the

* Khâna-zâdeh.

c 2

Koran *, and by all commentaries on that volume, to the manumission of slaves. Mahomed has said, " Unto such of your slaves as desire a written instrument, allowing them to redeem themselves, on paying a certain sum, write one, if ye know good in them, and give them of the riches of God, which he hath given you."

It is in obedience to this precept that pious Mahomedans often grant small pieces of land to a slave, or teach him a profession, that he may, through industry and frugality, attain the means of paying for his freedom, at the same time that he acquires habits which render him worthy of the great gift. Mahomedans are also encouraged to manumit their slaves by the law, which gives them a title, as residuary heir, to any property of which the person to whom they may have granted freedom dies possessed.

On one point the slaves in Mahomedan countries are on a footing with free females : they are only liable, for any crimes they commit, to suffer half the punishment to which a free man would be subject. This law proceeds on the ground of their

* Vide Sale's Koran, vol. II. p. 186.

not being supposed on a par, as to knowledge or social ties, with other parts of the community. The application, however, of this principle of justice to cases where the law awards death or amputation, has puzzled the wise Moullahs, or doctors, who have resorted to the usual remedy, of writing ponderous volumes upon the subject; but I do not learn that they have yet discovered a plan by which an offending woman or slave can be punished with the loss of half a life; or an operation be performed, which will leave them with a half-amputated limb.

To return to Muscat: I had visited it at all seasons; it was now winter, and the climate was pleasant; in summer the heat is intolerable. Shut out by the hills from every breeze, except that which blows directly into the narrow entrance of the cove, there is seldom a breath of air; and the reflection of the sun, from the bare rocks and white fortifications which overhang the town and harbour, produces a temperature, which is described by a Persian poet as giving to a panting sinner a lively anticipation of his future destiny!

The young Imam, Syed Sayed, was absent on an expedition; but I regretted this the less, as I had seen his father, who was, in-simplicity of manners, good sense, and courage, the equal of his deserving son.

Among the first who came on board, I was pleased to see my old friend, Mahomed Gholoum. Being a good seaman, he had, on the former mission in the year 1800, acted as our pilot from Muscat to Ormus. He was now advanced to be a pilot of the state, being one of the principal ministers of the young Imam, of whose character he spoke in high praise. " His father," said he, " was a brave man; he was killed in battle; and if his son goes on exposing himself every where, he will be killed also. He will regret much not seeing the Envoy, of whose kindness to him when a boy he retains a grateful recollection; for he preserves with great care the model of a seventy-four gun ship, with which he was presented by him."

Mahomed Gholoum was not changed by his prosperity, but retained all the frankness and manliness of an Arab sailor. We had many old stories, and at one, in which he was a prominent actor, he laughed very heartily. He had wished to take our vessel, the Bombay frigate, to the southward of

Ormus; but as we neared that island, the wind headed us, as the sailors call it, at the same time that it increased to a gale, and our pilot told the captain we had nothing left but to run for the harbour we desired to make, by steering between the island and the Persian shore. We did so; the weather became worse—it blew a hurricane; the channel, which is narrow, was missed, and we touched on a mud-bank, where the ship settled for a moment, and the waves dashed over her. The captain ordered more sail, to try and force her through the mud, exclaiming at the same time, " I would rather give a lac of rupees than lose the Company's ship." " Never mind the Company's ship," said a passenger, " so you land us safe." The seaman in the chains kept heaving the lead, and calling " Quarter less three." " What is the use of your quarter less three," said an impatient landsman, " when the ship is aground?" " That 's the captain's business, not mine," said the unconcerned Jack, and again he hove, and again he called " Quarter less three." At this moment my attention was drawn to my friend Mahomed Gholoum, who was appalled by an Irish officer's

exclaiming, " I do not understand your vile lingo;
but I will cut your throat (and he sawed with his
finger across his windpipe to make him comprehend
what he meant), I will cut your throat, you igno-
ramus, for drowning of gentlemen in this rascally
sea."

As these scenes were passing, the press of sail
which had been put upon our vessel forced her over
the bank: a few minutes more saw us safe in the
harbour of Ormus, and all our danger forgotten.
Mahomed Gholoum, quite exhausted, had, soon
after we anchored, fallen asleep on a couch in the
captain's cabin; but he was dreaming of past events,
and when I shook him, to make him rise to partake of supper, he started up, and with a wild look
called out " How many fathom have you ?"   We
told him to take his seat, and we would teach him,
Mahomedan as he was, to fathom a bowl.

Soon after our arrival at Muscat we were visited
by men of all nations and colours. I was principally attracted by the appearance and manners
of some Arabs from the interior, who were brought
on board by their countrymen to see an English
ship of war. Their figures were light and elastic,

their countenances expressed quickness and energy. The most remarkable of their features were their dark rolling eyes, which perhaps struck me more from their wandering rapidly from one object to another, glistening with wonder at all they saw. A good telescope happened to be placed so as to give a complete view of one of the farthest fortifications. I called an Arab to look through it, and he did so for about a minute, then gazed with the most eager attention at me, and, without saying a word, dashed over the ship's side. When the boat he was in got to a little distance, he exclaimed, " You are magicians, and I now see how you take towns ; that thing (pointing to the telescope), be they ever so far off, brings them as near as you like." We were much amused with his simplicity, but no arguments could prevail on him to return and receive such a lesson on optics as might dispel his delusion in supposing us to be adepts in the black art.

The Arabs at Muscat gave a luxuriant description of some beautiful valleys about twenty miles from that town ; but the result of minute inquiry forced us to conclude that the green meadows and

clear streams they described owed much of their
value to their rarity, and that the title of Arabia
the Happy is rather founded on the barrenness of
the far greater part of this renowned land, than on
any thing wonderful either in the climate or pro-
ductions of the tract to which it is applied.

CHAPTER III.

WHEN we had fairly entered the Persian Gulf, I found myself on classic ground, where all the wonderful adventures of Sinbad the sailor were, what a genuine Yankee would call, located. I sent for an Arabian servant called Khudâdâd, and asked him who were the inhabitants of the barren shore of Arabia that we saw. He answered with apparenta larm—"They are of the sect of Wahâbees, and are called Jouassimee; but God preserve us from them, for they are monsters. Their occupation is piracy, and their delight murder; and to make it worse, they give you the most pious reasons for every villany they commit. They abide by the letter of the sacred volume, rejecting all commentaries and traditions. If you are their captive, and offer all you possess to save your life, they say 'No! it is written in the Koran, that it is unlawful to plunder the living, but we are not prohibited in that sacred work from stripping the dead;' so saying,

they knock you on the head. But then," continued
Khudâdâd, " that is not so much their fault, for
they are descended from a Houl, or monster, and
they act according to their nature."

I begged he would inform me about their descent.
He seemed surprised at my ignorance, and said it
was a story that he thought was known to every
one in the world, but proceeded to comply with my
request.

" An Arab fisherman," said he, " who lived in a
village on the Persian Gulf, not far from Gombroon,
being one day busy at his usual occupation, found
his net so heavy that he could hardly drag it on
shore. Exulting in his good fortune, he exerted all
his strength : but judge of his astonishment, when,
instead of a shoal of fish, he saw in his net an animal of the shape of a man, but covered with hair.
He approached it with caution ; but finding it harm-
less, carried it to his house, where it soon became a
favourite ; for, though it could speak no language,
and utter no sound except ' houl, houl,' (from
whence it took its name), it was extremely docile
and intelligent ; and the fisherman, who possessed
some property, employed it to guard his flocks.

" It happened one day, that a hundred Persian horsemen, clothed in complete armour, came from the interior, and began to drive away the sheep. The Houl, who was alone, and had no arms but a club, made signs for them to desist; but they only scoffed at his unnatural appearance, till he slew one or two who approached too near him. They now attacked him in a body; but his courage and strength were surpassed by his activity, and while all fell who came within his reach, he eluded every blow of his enemies; and they fled after losing half their numbers.

" The fisherman and his neighbours, when they heard of the battle, hastened to the aid of the faithful Houl, whom they found in possession of the horses, clothes, and arms of the vanquished Persians. An Arab of the village, struck with his valour, and casting an eye of cupidity at the wealth he had acquired, offered him the hand of his daughter, who was very beautiful, and she, preferring good qualities to outward appearance, showed no reluctance to become the bride of this kind and gallant monster. Their marriage was celebrated with more pomp than was ever before known in the village;

and the Houl, who was dressed in one of the richest
suits of the Persians he had slain, and mounted on
one of their finest horses, looked surprisingly well.
He was quite beside himself with joy, playing such
antics, and exhibiting such good humour, strength,
and agility, that his bride, who had at first been
pitied, became the envy of every fisherman's daughter. She would have been more so, could they
have foreseen the fame to which she was destined.
She had four sons, from whom are descended the
four tribes of Ben Jouassim, Ben Ahmed, Ben Na-
sir, and Ben Saboohil, who are to this day known
by the general name of Ben Houl, or the children
of Houl. They are all fishermen, boatmen, and
pirates, and live chiefly at sea, inheriting, it is
believed, the amphibious nature of their common
ancestor."

After this tale was concluded, I asked Khudâdâd
what kind of men inhabited those high mountains
which we saw rising on the Persian shores of the
gulf. Delighted at this second opportunity of
showing his knowledge, he replied, " They also are
robbers, but they are not so bad as the Jouassimee.
They refer their first settlement in these mountains

to the devil; but then they are the children of men,
and their nature is not diabolical though their deeds
are sometimes very like it."

On questioning Khudâdâd further, I found he
had the popular story taken from Firdousee *, and
that he kept pretty near to his text ; but I shall give
it in his own words :—" You have heard of Zohâk,
prince of Arabia ?"   I said I had.   " Well then,"
he continued, " you know, he was a very wicked
man. He conquered Jemsheed, king of Persia,
who was in those days deemed the most glorious
monarch on earth. After this great success Zohâk
was tempted by the devil, who allured him, under
the shape of a venerable old man, to kill his father,
that he might become King of Arabia as well as
Persia. In those days men lived on vegetable
diet ; but the devil, anxious to destroy as many of
the human race as he could, tempted Zohâk with
some new roasted eggs, and perceiving him to relish his food, proposed to cook him a dish of par-

* Firdousee is the first of the epic poets of Persia, and few countries can boast of a greater genius. His chief work, the Shâh-nâmeh,
or Book of Kings, contains, mixed with allegory and fable, almost all
the Persians know of their ancient history.

tridges and quails, with the flavour of which the
prince was so delighted, that he bade his friend ask
any favour he liked. The wily old man said all
he wished was to kiss the shoulders of his beloved
monarch. They were bared for that purpose ; but
no sooner had the infernal lips touched them, than
out sprang from each a hissing ravenous serpent,
and at the same time the venerable old man changed
to his natural shape, and disappeared in a thunder-
storm, exclaiming, that human brains alone would.
satisfy the monsters he had created, and that their
death would be followed by that of Zohâk.

" It fell out as the devil foretold : the serpents refused all other food, and, for a period, two victims
were daily slain to satisfy them. Those charged
with the preparation of this horrid repast, seeing
the devil's design, determined on frustrating it ; and
while they paraded before Zohâk and his serpents
the persons who were doomed to death, they sub-
stituted the brains of sheep, and sent their supposed
human victims to the mountains of Kerman and
Lauristan, where they increased, and became a
great people, and their descendants still inhabit
these hills. There can be no doubt," said Khu-

dâdâd, gravely, " of the truth of what I have told
you; for it is all written in a book, and a fine poem
made upon it, which is called the Shâh-nâmeh, or
Book of Kings."

Having acquired this correct information about
the shores of the gulf, I landed at Abusheher *, a
Persian seaport, celebrated as the mart of chintzes
and long-ells, of dates and asafœtida. We were
met on the beach by the whole population of the
town. What appeared to excite most admiration
was the light company of his majesty's 84th regi-
ment, whose uniform appearance caused no slight
wonder. Struck with their similarity of look, one
man exclaimed, " These fellows must all have had
the same father and mother !" " That cannot be,"
said another, " for they must all have been born
on the same day." " They are proper devils,
I 'll warrant them," said an old woman, who had
been looking at them very attentively. They had
now received the order to march, and the regu-
larity with which their feet moved was a new subject of surprise. An old merchant, called Hajee

* Abusheher is the proper name, but it is better known to Europeans by the abbreviated appellation of Bushire.

Ismael, whose life had been spent amongst his accounts, and who delighted in every thing that was
regular, stood at a corner as they passed in files,
and kept saying, as he noted them with his fingers,
" correct *, correct, correct." Take it all in all, our
landing seemed to give great pleasure to the men,
women, and children of the port of Abusheher.

We had not been on shore a week before two
events occurred, one of which showed what the
Persians thought of us, and the other taught us
what we should think of them.

Before the year 1800 no political mission from
an European nation had visited the court of Persia
for a century ; but the English, though only known
in that kingdom as merchants, had fame as soldiers,
from the report of their deeds in India. An officer
of one of the frigates, who had gone ashore to visit
the Envoy, when mounted on a spirited horse, af-
forded no small entertainment to the Persians by
his bad horsemanship. Next day the man who
supplied the ship with vegetables, and who spoke a
little English, met him on board and said, " Don't

---

* " Hissab," the Persian word, literally means an account ; meta-
phorically, " correct, or according to a just account."

be ashamed, sir, nobody knows_you : bad rider ! I
tell them, you, like all English, ride well, but that
time they see you, very drunk !"   We were much
amused at this conception of our national character.
The Persian thought it would have been a reproach
for a man of a warlike nation not to ride well, but
none for an European to get drunk.

The other occurrence was still more characteristic.
The Envoy or Elchee *, as the Persians called him,
had, among other plans for doing good, one for
the introduction of potatoes.   Among those who
listened to him, and applauded his disinterested
intentions to benefit Persia, was a fat, smooth-faced
young merchant, who obtained a promise of a considerable quantity of potatoes for seed, having (according to his own report) rented a large piece of ground,
that he might be an humble instrument in the hands
of the British Representative for doing good.   The
latter, pleased with his zeal, honoured this excellent
man with such particular attention, that, conceiving
himself a prime favourite, he ventured one day to
suggest that " As the season was too far advanced
for the potatoe-garden that year, it would not be

* Elchee means embassador or representative of a foreign nation.

unworthy of the Elchee's wonted liberality to com-
mute his intended present for a pair of pistols, or a
piece of British broadcloth." This premature dis-
closure of the real object of this professed improver
of the soil produced no little ridicule, in which his
countrymen, who were jealous of the favour he had
enjoyed, joined most heartily. He was known till
the day of his death, which happened three years
ago, by the name of Potatoes. It is satisfactory to
add, that the plan for introducing this valuable root
did not fail; they were found to flourish at Abusheher, where they are called " Malcolm's * plum,"
after the Elchee, who looks to the accident which
gave his name to a useful vegetable as one of his
best chances of enduring fame.

The English factory, which had long been at
Gombroon, had been removed some years before
to Abusheher. All the old servants had accompanied it, and one, of the name of Suffer, had recently died, of whom I was delighted to hear, from
the best authority, an anecdote, which did credit to
the kindness of our countrymen, while it showed
that even in this soil, good usage will generate strong

* Alou, e, Malcolm.

and lasting attachment. When poor Suffer, who had been fifty years a servant in the factory, was on his death-bed, the English doctor ordered him a glass of wine. He at first refused it, saying, " I cannot take it; it is forbidden in the Koran." But after a few moments he begged the doctor to give it him, saying, as he raised himself in his bed, " Give me the wine; for it is written in the same volume, that all you unbelievers will be excluded from Paradise; and the experience of fifty years teaches me to prefer your society in the other world, to any place unto which I can be advanced with my own countrymen." He died a few hours after this sally, which I was glad to observe proved of value to his son, a rough-looking lad named Derveish, who was introduced by the Resident to the Envoy, at the time the former told the story of the father's attachment. Derveish was taken into service, and I have watched his gradual advancement till he has become the proprietor of a large boat, which is the ne plus ultra of the ambition of an Abusheheree.

The natives of this place are almost all of Arab race, and fond of the sea; a propensity the more remarkable, as it is in such strong contrast with the

disposition of the Persians, of whom all classes
have an unconquerable antipathy to that element.
But this is not the only characteristic distinction
between these classes of men, who appear to agree
in nothing but in dwelling in the same town.   The
Persians, who have been tempted by the hope of
gain to exchange the fine climate of the elevated
plains of the interior, for the sea-ports on the edge
of the sultry desert, which forms the shores of the
gulf, retain all the smooth pliant manners of their
country ; and they look with disgust on what they
deem the rude barbarous habits of the Arabians,
who are the great body of the inhabitants of this
track, and who can scarcely be distinguished, either
in look or sentiment, from their kindred on the opposite shore.

A remarkable instance of the difference of character, between the lower orders of these two classes,
occurred one morning, when the Envoy was preparing a match, to be run by a beautiful English
greyhound called Venus, and a strong Arabian dog
named Kessâb, or the Butcher. He was giving
directions to his master of the chase, Hyder, and
expressing his sanguine hopes of Venus's success ;

Mahomed Beg, a tall well-dressed Persian groom, assented to all his anticipations, saying, " What pretensions can that Arab dog have to run with the beautiful greyhound of the Elchee ?"

Others joined in the same language, and the opinion appeared general, when an Arab, called Gherreeba*, whose pay was only four piastres † a month, whose chequered turban and cloth round his middle were not worth one, and whose occupation was sitting all day exposed to the sun, watering some grass screens that were placed against the door of the house to exclude the heat—darted up, and, with an eye of fire and the most marked energy, exclaimed, " By the all-powerful God, the Arab dog will triumph ‡ !"

Gherreeba was for the moment the representative of the feelings of his country. The parasites around stood watching the Elchee, and were not a little mortified when they heard him applaud the honest

* Gherreeb means poor—this man was really so; but it is not unusual to meet Mahomedans, who are remarkable for their rank, pride, or wealth, with names of similar character, that have been given by their mothers in a spirit of religious humility.

† The value of a piastre is about twenty pence.

‡ Billâh il azeem yadhfar al Arab.

warmth and manly independence of the poor Arab,
who was invited to witness the trial. It ended, like
most similar trials, in each party being convinced
that their own favourite was, or ought to have been,
the winner. The dogs ran as usual beautifully:
Venus was by far the fleetest; but the chase, which
was after a half grown antelope, proved long, and
the strength of the Butcher prevailed towards the
close. It is, however, justice to the deer species,
while we are praising the canine, to add, that the
antelope beat them both.

CHAPTER IV.

CAMP AT ABUSHEHER—HORSES—ABDULLA AGA—
ANECDOTE OF ARAB.

Soon after we arrived at Abusheher our camp looked like a fair for horses and mules. It was necessary to mount, not only the Elchee and his suite, but his escort of English and Indian cavalry, and all the servants, public and private; for in Persia nobody walks. To suit the different persons of our party animals of different descriptions were wanted; from the coarse Persian galloway* to the Arabian of pure strain†, many of which are bred on the Persian shore, with as much attention to preserve the original blood, as imported from Arabia, as could be shown in the first race-studs in England.

Hyder, the Elchee's master of the chase, was the person who imparted knowledge to me on all subjects relating to Arabian horses. He would descant

---

* Yaboo.

† *Regee Pâk*, the term by which these high-bred animals are distinguished, means literally " pure veins."

by the hour on the qualities of a colt that was yet
untried, but which, he concluded, must possess all
the perfections of its sire and dam, with whose
histories, and that of their progenitors, he was well
acquainted. Hyder had shares in five or six famous
brood mares; and he told me a mare was sometimes divided amongst ten or twelve Arabs, which
accounted for the groups of half naked fellows
whom I saw watching, with anxiety, the progress
made by their managing partner in a bargain for
one of the produce. They often displayed, on these
occasions, no small violence of temper; and I have
more than once observed a party leading off their
ragged colt in a perfect fury, at the blood of
Daghee or Shumehtee, or some renowned sire or
grandsire, being depreciated by an inadequate offer,
from an ignorant Indian or European.

The Arabs place still more value on their mares
than on their horses; but even the latter are sometimes esteemed beyond all price. When the Envoy,
returning from his former mission, was encamped
near Bagdad, an Arab rode a bright bay horse, of
extraordinary shape and beauty, before his tent,
till he attracted his notice. On being asked if he

would sell him—" What will you give me?" said
he. " It depends upon his age; I suppose he is
past five?" " Guess again," was the reply. " Four."
" Look at his mouth," said the Arab with a smile.
On examination he was found rising three, this,
from his size and perfect symmetry, greatly en-
hanced his value. The Envoy said, " I will give
you fifty tomans *." " A little more, if you please,"
said the fellow, apparently entertained. " Eighty!
—a hundred!" He shook his head and smiled.
The offer came at last to two hundred tomans!
" Well," said the Arab, seemingly quite satisfied,
" you need not tempt me any farther—it is of no
use; you are a fine Elchee; you have fine horses,
camels, and mules, and I am told you have loads of
silver and gold: now," added he, " you want my
colt, but you shall not have him for all you have
got." So saying, he rode off to the desert, whence
he had come, and where he, no doubt, amused his
brethren with an account of what had passed between him and the European Envoy.

Inquiry was made of some officers of the Pasha
of Bagdad respecting this young man; they did not

* A toman is a nominal coin nearly the value of a pound sterling.

know him, but conjectured that, notwithstanding his homely appearance, he was the son or brother of a chief, or perhaps himself the head of a family; and such Arabs, they said, when in comparative affluence, no money could bribe to sell a horse like the one described.

I was one day relating the above story to Abdulla Aga, the former governor of Bussorah, who was at Abusheher, having been obliged to fly from Turkey. He told me that, when in authority, he several times had great trouble in adjusting disputes among Arab tribes, regarding a horse or mare which had been carried off by one of them from another; not on account of the value of the animals, that having been often offered ten-fold, but from jealousy of their neighbour's becoming possessed of a breed of horses which they desired to remain exclusively in their own tribe. An Arab Shaikh or chief, he told me, who lived within fifty miles of Bussorah, had a favourite breed of horses. He lost one of his best mares, and could not for a long time discover whether she was stolen or had strayed. Some time afterwards, a young man of a different tribe, who had long wished to marry his daughter, but had always been rejected by the Shaikh, obtained the lady's consent and eloped with her. The Shaikh and his followers pursued; but the lover and his mistress, mounted on the same horse, made a wonderful march, and escaped. The old chief swore that the fellow was either mounted upon the devil or the favourite mare he had lost. After his return he found, on inquiry, the latter was the case ; that the lover was the thief of his mare as well as of his daughter, and that he had stolen the one for the purpose of carrying off the other. He was quite gratified to think he had not been beaten by a horse of another breed, and was easily reconciled to the young man in order that he might recover the mare, which appeared an object about which he was more solicitous than his daughter.

Abdulla Aga is a man in whose company I take great pleasure. His understanding is vigorous and strong, and he has sufficient knowledge of the English character to speak his sentiments with freedom and confidence. I shall give the substance of a conversation I had with him about two weeks after my arrival, regarding the present condition of Persia and Turkey, with the resources and character of both which states he is intimately acquainted. Speaking of Turkey, he said he had no idea of its having the power to resist the slightest attack; and, he believed, if left alone, it would soon fall to pieces of itself.—" I am myself a Turk, and know my countrymen well: from the Grand Signior to the lowest peasant in the empire, they are alike devoid of public virtue and patriotism ; and that spirit of religion, which has long been the only bond of union that has kept this unwieldy state together, is every day becoming fainter; and while the Wahâbees are making converts of the inhabitants of Arabia and Syria, the provinces of Turkey in Europe are relaxing from their religious zeal, and becoming every day more ripe for the rule of those Christian nations, under whose power they must soon fall."

I could not help saying I thought he drew an overcharged picture of the weak and distracted state of his country. " You will soon see," he said, " whether I am right or wrong. No man, whatever may be his rank, looks beyond his beard in Turkey: if he can find any expedient that gives him a prospect of its growing grey in quiet, he is content; and where all are so decidedly selfish in their views, who is to provide for the safety of the state, to guard which there must be some common sentiment of union ?"

"What think you of Persia?" I asked. "Why, twenty times worse than of Turkey," replied he; "because they are to the full as devoid of every public principle, and much more ignorant. Believe me, you will soon be satisfied that they deserve this character. Can there be a doubt at the present moment, how they ought to act between you and the French? and yet you will be able to settle nothing with them that is in the least satisfactory without heavy bribes or harsh measures. The latter," he added, "will be the wisest in the present instance; for to feed their cupidity is only to whet their appetite, and to encourage them in a course that will, in its result, prove as injurious to these short-sighted fools as to the interests of the English government."

"The Elchee's intentions are so friendly," I observed in reply, "and his wishes so correspond with their true interests, that they must, I think, meet them, when all the advantages are explained." "Before you anticipate success from such an explanation, you should be certain that those to whom you speak have sense to comprehend you, which the Persians certainly have not. They think of nothing at this moment but the Russians, with whom they have discovered they are not able to contend. The French pretend to relieve them from this formidable danger, which they have not themselves the courage to face; and they cling to this promise without ever considering how far those who make it have the means of performing it. They neither understand the nature nor distance of the resources of England or France, and are consequently incapable of forming a correct idea of the comparative power which those states possess of aiding or injuring them. They know that Bombay is within a month's sail, Madras six weeks, and Calcutta two months; and they believe you have some ships at these places; but even of these they have no clear idea; and as to Europe, they are as ignorant as an Abyssinian."

" Assuredly," said I, " you underrate their knowledge." " I do not," said Abdulla; " they are worse than I have painted them, and their ignorance is so fortified by pride that there is no hope of their amendment. Why (said he, with animation), what can you expect from men who are ignorant of the surface of the globe? There," said he, pointing to a rude Turkish book on geography, which lay near him, and appeared to be a translation from an old geographical grammar—" there is the only source of my knowledge, which does not place me on a par with one of your school-boys of twelve years of age, and yet I am a wonder among these fools, who are astonished at the extent of my information in this branch of science."

Though I think it is a very deep and wise observation of that arch politician Machiavel, that the report of a man who has fled his country should not be implicitly trusted, as there must be a bias in his mind to depreciate what he has been obliged to abandon: still there is much truth in the picture which Abdulla drew of Turkey, and his description of the Persians was not greatly exaggerated. The knowledge of that nation is limited to what they see before them, and their ideas of other States are very indistinct and confused, and consequently liable to frequent fluctuations and changes. All ranks in Persia are brought up to admire show and parade; and they are more likely to act from the dictates of

imagination and vanity than of reason and judgment. Their character was well drawn by Mahomed Nubbee Khan, the late Ambassador to
India : " If you wish my countrymen to understand you, speak to their eyes, not their ears."

My conversation with Abdulla Aga was interrupted by the arrival of a Medical Gentleman, who
had long resided at Abusheher, and who was not
more remarkable for skill in his profession than
a kindness of heart, which led him to devote his
time to the poor inhabitants of the country who
sought his aid. He had just been setting the broken
leg of an Arab, of whom he gave us a very characteristic anecdote.

" The patient," the doctor said, " complained
more of the accident which had befallen him than
I thought becoming in one of his tribe. This I remarked to him, and his answer was truly amusing.
' Do not think, doctor, I should have uttered one
word of complaint if my own high-bred colt, in a
playful kick, had broke both my legs ; but to have
a bone broken by a brute of a jackass is too bad,
and I will complain.' "

This distinction of feeling, as to the mode in which

bones are broken, is not confined to the Arabs.   I
once met an artillery-man, after an action in India,
with his arm shattered, who was loudly lamenting
his bad fortune.   I pointed in an upbraiding manner to some fine fellows on the ground, whose luck
had been worse.   " It is not the wound, sir," he
retorted, in a passion, " of which I complain : had
I lost a limb by a cannon-ball I should not have said
a word ; but to lose one by a rascally rocket would
make any one mad !"

CHAPTER V.

WE were kept several weeks at Abusheher; and
among other amusements by which we beguiled the
tedium of our sojourn at this dull seaport, were
those of hunting and hawking; which, according
to the Nimrods of our party, is nowhere found in
greater perfection: but as the mode of killing the
game differs essentially from that of other countries,
I shall describe it, that such sportsmen as can read
may judge of its merits.

The huntsmen proceed to a large plain, or rather
desert, near the sea-side: they have hawks and greyhounds; the former carried in the usual manner, on
the hand of the huntsman; the latter led in a leash
by a horseman, generally the same who carries the
hawk. When the antelope is seen, they endeavour
to get as near as possible; but the animal, the mo-

ment it observes them, goes off at a rate that seems
swifter than the wind ; the horsemen are instantly
at full speed, having slipped the dogs. If it is a
single deer, they at the same time fly the hawks ;
but if a herd, they wait till the dogs have fixed on
a particular antelope. The hawks, skimming along
near the ground, soon reach the deer, at whose head
they pounce in succession, and sometimes with a
violence that knocks it over. At all events, they
confuse the animal so much as to stop its speed in
such a degree that the dogs can come up ; and in
an instant men, horses, dogs, and hawks, surround
the unfortunate deer, against which their united
efforts have been combined. The part of the chase
that surprised me most was the extraordinary
combination of the hawks and the dogs, which
throughout seemed to look to each other for aid.
This, I was told, was the result of long and skilful
training.

The antelope is supposed to be the fleetest qua-
druped on earth, and the rapidity of the first burst
of the chase I have described is astonishing. The
run seldom exceeds three or four miles, and often is
not half so much. A fawn is an easy victory ; the

doe often runs a good chase, and the buck is seldom
taken. The Arabs are indeed afraid to fly their
hawks at the latter, as these fine birds in pouncing
frequently impale themselves on its sharp horns.

The hawks used in this sport are of a species
that I have never seen in any other country. This
breed, which is called Cherkh, is not large, but of
great beauty and symmetry.

Another mode of running down the antelope is
practised here, and still more in the interior of
Persia. Persons of the highest rank lead their
own greyhounds in a long silken leash, which passes
through the collar, and is ready to slip the moment
the huntsman chooses. The well-trained dog goes
alongside the horse, and keeps clear of him when at
full speed, and in all kinds of country. When a
herd of antelopes is seen, a consultation is held, and
the most experienced determine the point towards
which they are to be driven. The field (as an
English sportsman would term it) then disperse,
and while some drive the herd in the desired direction, those with the dogs take their post on
the same line, at the distance of about a mile from
each other; one of the worst dogs is then slipped

at the herd, and from the moment he singles out
an antelope the whole body are in motion. The
object of the horsemen who have greyhounds is to
intercept its course, and to slip fresh dogs, in succession, at the fatigued animal. In rare instances
the second dog kills. It is generally the third or
fourth ; and even these, when the deer is strong,
and the ground favourable, often fail. This sport,
which is very exhilarating, was the delight of the
late King of Persia, Aga Mahomed Khan, whose
taste is inherited by the present Sovereign.

The novelty of these amusements interested me,
and I was pleased, on accompanying a party to a
village, about twenty miles from Abusheher, to see
a species of hawking peculiar, I believe, to the
sandy plains of Persia, on which the Hubara*, a
noble species of bustard, is found on almost bare
plains, where it has no shelter but a small shrub

---

* The Hubara usually weighs from seven to eleven pounds. On
its head is a tuft of black and white feathers ; the back of the head
and neck are spotted black ; the side of the head and throat are white,
as well as the under part of the body ; the breast is slate-coloured ;
the feathers of the wing are greenish brown, speckled with black ; the
bill of a very dark grey ; and on each side of the neck is a large and
handsome tuft of feathers, black and white alternately.

called geetuck. When we went in quest of them
we had a party of about twenty, all well mounted.
Two kinds of hawks are necessary for this sport;
the first, the Cherkh (the same which is flown at
the antelope), attacks them on the ground, but will
not follow them on the wing; for this reason, the
Bhyree, a hawk well known in India, is flown the
moment the Hubara rises.

As we rode along in an extended line, the men
who carried the Cherkhs every now and then un-
hooded and held them up, that they might look
over the plain. The first Hubara we found af-
forded us a proof of the astonishing quickness
of sight of one of the hawks; he fluttered to be
loose, and the man who held him gave a whoop,
as he threw him off his hand, and set off at full
speed. We all did the same. At first we only
saw our hawk skimming over the plain, but soon
perceived, at a distance of more than a mile, the
beautiful speckled Hubara, with his head erect
and wings outspread, running forward to meet his
adversary. The Cherkh made several unsuccessful
pounces, which were either evaded or repelled by
the beak or wings of the Hubara, which at last

found an opportunity of rising, when a Bhyree was instantly flown, and the whole party were again at full gallop. We had a flight of more than a mile, when the Hubara alighted, and was killed by another Cherkh, who attacked him on the ground. This bird weighed ten pounds. We killed several others, but were not always successful, having seen our hawks twice completely beaten, during the two days we followed this fine sport.

The inhabitants of the country over which we hunted are all Arabs. They live, like their brethren in other parts, almost entirely on camels' milk and dates. Their care appears limited to the preservation of the animal and the propagation of the tree, which yield what they account the best of this world's luxuries; and these not only furnish this lively race of men with food, but with almost all the metaphors in which their language abounds. Of this we had an amusing instance: amongst others who accompanied the Elchee on this sporting expedition, was a young Officer, who measured six feet seven inches; he, like others, had lain down to take an hour's repose, between our morning and evening hunt. An old Arab who was desired to

awake him, smiling, said to his servant, " Entreat
your date-tree to rise." We had a hearty laugh at
our friend, who was not at first quite reconciled to
this comparison of his commanding stature to the
pride of the desert.

If we were amused by the field diversions of the
Persians and Arabs, they were equally so with
our mode of hunting. The Elchee had brought a
few couples of English fox-hounds, intending them
as a present to the Heir-apparent, Abbas Meerza.
With this small pack we had several excellent runs.
One morning we killed a fox, after a very hard
chase; and while the rest of the party were exulting in their success, cutting off poor reynard's
brush, praising the hounds, adding some two feet
to a wall their horses had cleared, laughing at
those who had got tumbles, and recounting many a
hair-breadth escape, I was entertained by listening
to an Arab peasant, who, with animated gestures,
was narrating to a group of his countrymen all he
had seen of this noble hunt. " There went the
fox," said he, pointing with a crooked stick to a
clump of date-trees; " there he went at a great
rate; I hallooed, and hallooed, but nobody heard

me, and I thought he must get away; but when
he was quite out of sight, up came a large spotted
dog, and then another and another; they all had
their noses on the ground, and gave tongue, whow,
whow, whow, so loud that I was frightened:—away
went these devils, who soon found the poor animal;
after them galloped the Faringees *, shouting and
trying to make a noise louder than the dogs: no
wonder they killed the fox among them; but it is
certainly fine sport. Our Shaikh has no dogs like
these." The last remark was assented to by all
present, and the possession of a breed of dogs,
which their Shaikh had not, added not a little,
in the eyes of those peasants, to the character of
the Mission.

We were now busy preparing to leave Abusheher.
Before we took our departure, the Shaikh gave the
Elchee and his Suite an entertainment. Among other
subjects of conversation at this feast, the name of the
Derveish Abdulla, who had some years before visited
that port, and sailed for India, was mentioned. I
smiled as they related stories of his sanctity and
learning, and still more as I found different par-

* Faringee, which is a corruption of Frank, is the name given to
an European over all Asia.

ties, a Turk, a Persian, and an Arab, contending
for the honour their country derived from his belonging to it. " You have only to hear him speak,
and repeat poetry," said Hajee Ismael, " to be certain he is a Persian." " It is his recital of passages of the Koran, that convinces me he is an
Arab," said the Shaikh. " You may say what you
like," said Abdulla Aga, " but no man but a native of Turkey ever spoke Turkish like Derveish
Abdulla."

At this part of the conversation I put in my
word, and said, " Really, Gentlemen, you are all
mistaken ; the far-famed Derveish you mention is a
Frenchman, his real name is Tollemache, and I
know him well." It was not a mere smile of in-
credulity with which they listened. The remark
I had made, while it received not the least credit,
excited unpleasant feelings, and a friend near me
whispered that it was better to abstain from the
subject.

The following is a short history of this remarkable individual, who has attained such a perfection
in the languages and manners of the natives of
Asia as to deceive the most learned.

Mons. Tollemache, the son of a Dragoman at

Constantinople, was many years ago recommended to Mr. Warren Hastings, who patronized him ; but a quarrel, in which he was involved, at Calcutta, led to his leaving that city and going to the north-western part of India, from whence he went into the countries of Cabool, Khorassan, and Persia, and was lost trace of by his European friends for twelve years. His latter name in Persia was the Derveish Abdulla, under which he became renowned for his piety and learning. He had officiated as first reader of prayers * before the late King, who ho-noured him with his favour. He came to Abu-sheher, from whence he went to Surat, where, after his overtures of service to the English government had been refused, he proceeded to the Isle of France, and is mentioned in Lord Wellesley's notes as the person employed there with Tippoo Sultan's Am-bassadors. On proceeding afterwards to the Red Sea he was made prisoner by Admiral Blanket, and sent to Bombay, where I became acquainted with him at the house of a friend with whom he resided.

The memory of Tollemache was stored with rare Persian poems and songs : his conversation

* Paish Namaz.

was, from his various knowledge, very entertaining. Of his power to assume any Asiatic character, the following anecdote will suffice. He
had been dilating on his success in deceiving natives of the countries through which he passed, and
observed me to be rather incredulous. I had not
remarked his leaving the room some minutes before
I did, but, when driving out of the gate, I was so
annoyed by the importunities of a Mahomedan mendicant, who was almost naked, that I abused him,
and threatened to use my whip, if he did not desist, when the fellow burst into a fit of laughter,
and asked me if I so soon forgot my acquaintances?
I could hardly credit my eyes and ears on recog-
nising Tollemache; and the recollection of this occurrence prevented me saying more to my friends
at the Shaikh's party, whom I left in the belief that
the holy Abdulla was a saint upon earth.

The first march from Abusheher we had to pass
over a desert plain of considerable extent, on which
I amused myself by watching narrowly the various
changes, as we were near or remote from it, of that
singular vapour, called by the French Mirage, and
by the Arabs and Persians Sirab.

The influence of this vapour in changing the

figure of objects is very extraordinary ; it sometimes gives to those seen through it the most fantastical shapes ; and, as a general effect, I think it always appears to elevate and make objects seem much taller than they really are. A man, for instance, seen through it at the distance of a mile and a half upon the level plain appears to be almost as tall as a date-tree.

Its resemblance to water is complete, and justifies all the metaphors of poets, and their tales of thirsty and deluded travellers.

The most singular quality of this vapour is its power of reflection. When a near observer is a little elevated, as on horseback, he will see trees and other objects reflected as from the surface of a lake. The vapour, when seen at a distance of six or seven miles, appears to lie upon the earth like an opaque mass ; and it certainly does not rise many feet above the ground, for I observed, that while the lower part of the town of Abusheher was hid from the view, some of the more elevated buildings, and the tops of a few date-trees, were distinctly visible.

Among the presents for his majesty of Persia

were two light field-pieces, to which were attached
a select detachment of horse-artillery. Great care
was taken to equip this party in the best style; and
as they had a difficult march to perform, they were
sent in advance, under the tall officer who has been
already mentioned. Our third stage to Dalkhee
was so rough and stony, that we were alarmed lest
we should hear bad accounts of their progress; but
our fears were all dissipated by the reports of the
villagers.

" Their fathers," they said, " had never seen
such guns, nor such a young man as their Officer."
" Why," said an old Moullah, " I have often seen
our guns. They move only a few yards in an
hour, though dragged by a hundred oxen and a
hundred men, and at every step the air resounds
with ' Ya Allah ! ya Allah !' (O God! O God!)
my countrymen being obliged to invoke Heaven to
help them in their heavy work ; but your young
Officer (who is himself a wonder in size) jumps upon
his horse and cries ' tap, tap,' and away trot the
guns like feathers. We all came to look at him
and his guns, and stared till we were tired ; and
every one expressed his admiration. As for me, I

have commenced a poem upon the party." The
Elchee, who had been laughing, looked grave at
this threat of a kesseeda or ode ; for he is already
overwhelmed with such compositions : every man
in Persia who can make two lines rhyme in praise
of the Mission being anxious to change, as soon as
possible, the product of his imagination into solid
piastres.

All our baggage and camp equipage was carried
upon mules; and no country can boast of finer animals of this description than Persia. They carry
heavy burdens, and travel great distances, at a rate
of better than four miles an hour. They go in
strings ; and I was amused to see them, when at
the end of the march and unloaded, tied in circles,
going after each other, at their usual pace, till they
were cool.

The Khater-bashee, or master of the mules, is a
person of the first importance. This class of men
are generally known by the strength of their frame,
and, above all, of their lungs, which are continually
exercised in consigning man and beast to every
species of torment and evil, both in this world and
the next. On the first mission to Persia we had a

mule-driver called Hajee Hashem, who, from his
strength and temper, was the terror of caravans.
This man, on our second day's march, anxious to
unload his mules, refused to pay any attention to
the injunctions of Peter, the Elchee's steward, and
carelessly cast a box containing glass upon some
loose stones, at the hazard of breaking its contents.
Peter, who had been educated on board a man-of-
war, and was a very stout fellow, irritated beyond
bearing at this treatment of his pantry ware, seized
Hajee by the waist, and before he had time to
make an effort, cast him over the animal he had so
rudely unloaded; and while the astonished mule-
driver lay sprawling, and not yet knowing whether
his bones were broken, Peter, calling his interpreter,
a Persian servant, who had learned a little English
at Bombay—" Tell that fellow," he said, in a voice
which showed his rage was only half expended, " it
is lucky for him that his bones are not so brittle as
my glass, of which he will take better care another
time."

Having witnessed this scene, I anticipated a complaint to the Elchee; but what was my surprise to
learn, that Hajee Hashem had petitioned to be ex-

clusively attached, with his mules, to Peter's department! He was so; they continued always the best of friends; and no disappointment could be greater than that of the old Hajee, when he came to furnish cattle for the second mission, at finding his ally Peter was not of the party.

The ground of Hajee Hashem's attachment to his friend may be deemed extraordinary: but had the master muleteer been a historian, he might have pleaded high authority in his own country, for valuing another for superiority in the rough qualities in which he himself excelled.

The emperor of Constantinople, Mahmood the fifth, the great rival of Nadir Shah, desiring to humble the vanity of that conqueror, and knowing he valued himself more on his superior bodily power and stentorian voice than on any other qualities, selected, as an Envoy to Persia, a Porter of extraordinary personal strength and most powerful lungs.

The Envoy had merely charge of a letter, which he was told to deliver in person to the king, to require an answer, and return. The fame of this remarkable diplomatist preceded him; and Nadir was advised not to receive him, as his deputation

was deemed an insult. But curiosity overcame all
other considerations, and he was introduced one
day that there was a very full court.

When the Turk approached the throne, Nadir,
assuming his fiercest look, and exerting his voice to
the utmost, said, " What do you desire of me ?"
Almost all started, and the hall vibrated to the
sound ; but the Envoy, with an undaunted air, and
in a voice of thunder which made Nadir's appear
like the treble of a child, exclaimed, " Take that
letter, and give me an answer, that I may return
to my master."

The court were in amazement ; all eyes were
turned on Nadir, whose frowning countenance gradually relaxed into a smile, and, turning to his
courtiers, he said, " After all, the fellow certainly
has merit." He was outdone, but he could not
help, like Hajee Hashem, respecting in another the
qualities he valued in himself.

Nadir is stated to have retorted the intended insult, by saying to the Envoy, when he gave him
leave to depart, " Tell Mahmood I am glad to find
he has one man in his dominions, and has had the
good sense to send him here, that we may be satisfied of the fact."

CHAPTER VI.

THE Elchee, from the moment we landed in
Persia, has been lecturing us on the importance of
the conduct of every individual, as connected with
a just impression of the national character. " These
Persians," said he to us one day, " have no knowledge beyond their country; they understand no
language but their own and Arabic; and though
all the better classes read, the books to which they
have access afford them little if any information,
except of Asia. Europe, in fact, is only known
by name, and by general and confused accounts of
the fame of its nations, and their comparative greatness. They are, however," he added, " a very
keen and observing people, and full of curiosity.
In the absence of books, they will peruse us, and,
from what they hear and see, form their opinion of
our country. Let us take care, therefore, that no-

thing is found in the page but what is for the honour of England; and believe me that, with such a
people, more depends upon personal impressions
than treaties."

With these sentiments, every word and act was
shaped by him, and, so far as he could command
and influence them, by others, to raise the English
character. It was not enough that we were to give
an example of all kinds of good qualities, but we
were to be active and capable of fatigue, to show the
Persians we were soldiers. The Envoy or Elchee,
as they called him, happened to have a robust form,
and a passion for shooting and hunting. It was,
therefore, nothing more than an amusement to him
to ride fifty or sixty miles of a morning, that he
might surpass his Mehmandar or entertainer in
his own line, but it was far otherwise to many of
his suite. I did not like it ; and a near relation of
his, who was rather weak, and, like me, of sedentary
habits, used to inveigh bitterly against these " political rides," as he scoffingly termed them.   There
was, however, some sense in the Elchee's proceed-
ings, as I discovered, when an intimacy with our
old Mehmandar, Mahomed Sheriff Khan, a Burga-

shattee*, led to his showing me a journal he had written for the information of the court by whom he was deputed, in order to enable them to judge, by the aid of his observations, what kind of a person and nation they had to deal with. I shall transcribe the passage, which was literally as follows.

" The Elchee, and the English Gentlemen with him, rise at dawn of day ; they mount their horses and ride for two or three hours, when they come home and breakfast. From that time till four o'clock, when they dine, the Elchee is either looking at horses, conversing, reading, or writing ; he never lies down, and, if he has nothing else to do, he walks backwards and forwards before his tent-door, or within it. He sits but a short time at dinner, mounts his horse again in the evening, and when returned from his ride, takes tea, after which he converses, or plays at cards till ten o'clock, when he retires to rest ; and next day pursues nearly the same course.

" What I chiefly remark is, that neither he nor any of the Gentlemen sleep during the day, nor do

---

* Burgashattee is the name of a small Turkish tribe, of which this old nobleman was chief.

they ever, when the weather is warm, recline upon
carpets as we do.   They are certainly very restless
persons; but when it is considered that these habits cause their employing so much more time every
day in business, and in acquiring knowledge, than
his Majesty's subjects, it is evident that at the end
of a year they must have some advantage.   I can
understand, from what I see, better than I could
before, how this extraordinary people conquered
India.   My office is very fatiguing, for the Elchee,
though a good-natured man, has no love of quiet,
and it is my duty to be delighted with all he does,
and to attend him on all occasions."

This journal was written upon observations made
before we left Abusheher.   The poor old Mehmandar was compelled, soon after we marched, to
slack in his constant attendance; for, as the Elchee's
duty and inclination coincided, he was seldom satisfied with a stage of twenty or thirty miles, but
usually went out in the evening of the same day to
hunt, which, no doubt, made the desired impression,
and led the Persians in his Suite to think, if the
English, in very sport, so harassed their friends,
what would become of their enemies?

My friend, Mahomed Sheriff Khan, was, as appears from his journal, a keen observer. He had
the reputation of being a good soldier; but his distinguishing feature was pride in his condition, as
the chief of a tribe, and as representing, in his
person, a portion of the authority of the King of
Kings! This pride, however, which often flamed
forth in real or assumed rage, was much regulated
in its action by a regard for his own interests. He
was always civil to the Elchee, and those with him,
but to all upon whom his office gave him claims his
demeanour was haughty and overbearing, till soothed
by concession or bribes. I met the Mehmandar one
morning, with a man leading a beautiful Arab colt,
to which he pointed, saying, " That old scoundrel,
Shaikh Nasser (Governor of Abusheher), had very
nearly deprived me of that animal." " What!"
said I, " could he venture to take him from you?"
" No," said he; " the horse was his; but he had
concealed him so carefully that I was near going
away without getting him. I heard of him before
I left Shiraz, and have been on the search ever
since I came to Abusheher. I have just found him,
hidden in an inner room, covered with dirt: and

then to hear how the old fool whined about this colt
of his favourite Daghee*, as he called him.   He
meant him, he said, to mount his son, a puny
wretch, who was standing by, entreating me to listen
to his father's prayer, and not to take away their
only favourite; to save which, they offered several
useless animals and some money.   But I laughed
out loud," concluded. Mahomed Sheriff Khan,
stroking his grizzly beard, "and said, they knew
little of an old wolf like me, if they thought I was
to be moved by their bleating, or tricked by their
cunning.   Go," said I to the old Shaikh, "and
build a boat for that hopeful heir of yours; it will
befit him better than a horse like this, which is
only suited for a son of mine to ride upon."

I soon afterwards saw old Shaikh Nasser moving
slowly along, muttering his usual phrase, "There's
no harm done†: Persian scoundrels, Arab fools, all
will go to hell together! God is just!—Well, well,
there's no harm done."   I spoke to him—he took
no notice, but went to his usual seat to superintend

* A celebrated stud-horse of Shaikh Nasser.

† *Aibee na dared*, which is literally translated in the text, was
a phrase used by this old chief on every occasion.

some carpenters, who were building a vessel which had been on the stocks about seventy years; there his smothered passion found vent in the most virulent abuse of all his tribe who approached him. When I spoke to him some time afterwards, he seemed in better humour. " This ship," said he, pointing to the ribs of the rude vessel, " will be finished some day or other, and she will hold us all: There is no harm done."

Mahomed Sheriff Khan used to laugh at his own habits, which he deemed less personal than belonging to his condition. One day, when riding through the streets, he observed me looking significantly at his Turkuman horse stretching his long neck to seize some greens, which a man was carrying in a basket on his head—" He has learnt it *," said my friend, with a smile.

When I looked on the desert arid plains which lie between Abusheher and the mountains, and saw the ignorant, half-naked, swarthy men and women broiling under a burning sun, with hardly any food but dates, my bosom swelled with pity for their condition, and I felt the dignity of the human species

* *Amookhta ast.*

degraded by their contented looks. " Surely," said
I to Khojah Arratoon, an Armenian (known in
the mission by the name of ' Blue-beard *'), these
people cannot be so foolish as to be happy in this
miserable and uninstructed state.   They appear a
lively, intelligent race—can they be insensible to
their comparatively wretched condition ?   Do they
not hear of other countries ? have they no envy, no
desire for improvement ?"   The good old Armenian
smiled, and said, " No ; they are a very happy race
of people, and so far from envying the condition of
others, they pity them.   But," added he, seeing
my surprise, " I will give you an anecdote which
will explain the ground of this feeling.

" Some time since, an Arab woman, an inhabitant
of Abusheher, went to England † with the children
of a Mr. Beauman.   She remained in your country

* The nick-name of Blue-beard was given by some of the young
men of our party to our Treasurer, Khojah Arratoon, from that colour being one day predominant in the dye he had used to ornament
his beard.   This excellent man is now no more.

† This story has been told by Sir John Malcolm, in his history,
in illustration of some of his facts or opinions ; but he has taken this,
and many other equally good things, from me, without ever acknow-
ledging them ; I shall, therefore, stand on no ceremony when it suits
my purpose to reclaim my property.

four years. When she returned, all gathered round her to gratify their curiosity about England. ' What did you find there? is it a fine country? are the people rich—are they happy?' She an-swered, ' The country was like a garden; the people were rich, had fine clothes, fine houses, fine horses, fine carriages, and were said to be very wise and happy.' Her audience were filled with envy of the English, and a gloom spread over them, which showed discontent at their own condition. They were departing with this sentiment, when the woman happened to say, ' England certainly wants one thing.' ' What is that?' said the Arabs eagerly. ' There is not a single date-tree in the whole coun-try!' ' Are you sure?' was the general exclama-tion. ' Positive,' said the old nurse; ' I looked for nothing else all the time I was there, but I looked in vain.' This information produced an instanta-neous change of feeling among the Arabs: it was pity, not envy, that now filled their breasts; and they went away, wondering how men could live in a country where there were no date-trees!"

This anecdote was told me as I was jogging on the road, alongside my friend Blue-beard, on our

first march from Abusheher. I rode the remainder
of the way (ten good miles) without speaking a word,
but pondering on the seeming contradiction between
the wisdom of Providence and the wisdom of man.
I even went so far as to doubt the soundness of
many admirable speeches and some able pamphlets
I had read, regarding the rapid diffusion of knowledge. I changed to a calculating mood, and began
to think it was not quite honest, even admitting it
was wise, to take away what men possessed, of content and happiness, until you could give them an
equal or greater amount of the same articles.

Before leaving Abusheher we had received many
proofs of the favour of the Prince Regent of Shiraz.
Soon after our arrival at that place, a favourite
officer of his Guards brought a present of twelve
mule-loads of fruit. When this young man came
to pay his respects to the Elchee, Khojah Arratoon desired to withdraw. When asked the reason : " Why," said he, " the person who is deputed by the Prince is a Georgian, the son of my
next door neighbour in Teflis. When Aga Mahomed Khan plundered that city in 1797, he was
made a prisoner, with twenty or thirty thousand

young persons of both sexes; and having since
been compelled to become a Mahomedan, and now
enjoying high rank, he may be embarrassed at
seeing me." The Envoy said, " It does not signify,
you are my Treasurer, and must be present at the
visit of ceremony; depend upon it he will not
notice you." It was as predicted; the bearer of
the present, a very handsome young man, superbly
dressed, and of finished manners, appeared to have
no knowledge of Arratoon, though his eye rested on
him once or twice. When the visit was over, the
good Armenian could not contain himself: " The
vile Mahomedan wretch!" he exclaimed, " he has
lost sight and feeling, as well as religion and virtue. Have I given him sweetmeats so often, to be
stared at as a stranger? I should like to know who
was his father, that he should look down upon
me. It will be a mournful tale," he concluded,
"that I shall have to write to his mother, who is
in great distress, and who, poor deluded creature!
lives in hopes that there is still some good in this
dog of a son of hers." There was a mixture of
wounded pride, of disappointment, and humanity,
in Blue-beard's sentiments, that made them at once
amusing, and affecting.

He came, however, early next morning to the
Envoy with a very different countenance, and evidently deeply affected. " What injustice have I
not done," said he, " to that excellent young man!
He sent a secret messenger to me last night; and
when we met, ran to embrace me, and after telling me the short tale of his captivity, sufferings,
and subsequent advancement, inquired in the most
earnest manner after his mother.   He has not
only given a hundred tomans to relieve her immediate wants, but has settled that I am to be the
Agent for future remittances.   He informed me
that he recognised the friend of his youth, and never
had more difficulty than in the effort to appear a
stranger; but he explained his reasons for being so
cautious: he is not only a Mahomedan, but has married into a respectable family, and is a great favourite
with the Prince, and must, therefore, avoid any conduct that could bring the least shade of suspicion on
the sincerity of his faith or allegiance.   I shall make
his mother very happy," continued Blue-beard, who
was evidently quite flattered by the personal attention of the young Georgian, and the confidence
reposed in him; " for I will, when I send her the
tomans, tell her my conviction, that her son, what-

ever he may profess, is a Christian in his heart.
Indeed he must be so; for if he had been a true
Mahomedan he would have acted like one, and
have disowned, not supported, his mother, whom
he must consider an infidel."

The Prince Regent of Fars, or Persia Proper,
sent, soon after our arrival at Abusheher, a young
Nobleman of his own tribe, Hassan Khan Kajir, to
attend the Elchee as Mehmandar. My intimacy,
from old acquaintance, with Jaffier Khan, Governor
of Abusheher, led to his showing me the letter he
had received from his brother, the Prince's vizier,
regarding the reception of this personage. It is
so good a specimen of the minute attention the Persians give to forms that I translated it. Its contents were as follows:

" MY DEAR BROTHER,

          " HASSAN Khan Kajir, who is appointed
Mehmandar to General Malcolm, is a Nobleman of
the first rank and family. He will keep you informed of his progress. When he arrives at Dalkhee* he will send on this letter, and write you on

          * Fifty miles from Bushire.

the subject of his waiting upon the General, the day
he comes to camp. You will proceed to meet him,
with all the Garrison of Abusheher, as far as the
date-trees on the border of the desert. You will
accompany him to General Malcolm's tent, and,
when he leaves it, you will proceed with him to
his own tent, which must be pitched as the General
desires, on the right or left of his encampment. If
Hassan Khan Kajir arrives in the morning, you
will stay and breakfast with him; if in the evening,
you will dine with him. Your future attention will
be regulated by your politeness and good sense, and
you will always consider him as a Noble guest, who
should be entertained in a manner suitable to his
rank and the distinguished situation to which he is
appointed, of Mehmandar to General Malcolm."

The Mehmandar wrote a letter with this, in which
he explained to the Governor, as modestly as the
subject would admit, his own expectations. The
Governor was anxious to know how the Envoy
would receive him; and when told that two Officers
would meet him at a short distance from the camp,
and that the Escort would be drawn up before the
tent at which he alighted to salute him, his mind

was at rest, as he was sure such attention would be
gratifying to this sixteenth cousin of Majesty.

Hassan Khan made his appearance next day, and
proved to be a fine young man, about twenty-six
years of age, of excellent manners and handsome
in person, with grey eyes, and a very pleasing expression of countenance.   At this visit he was pro-
fuse in professions of the regard in which the King
and Prince held the Elchee, both of whom, he said,
were anxious for the advance of the Mission.

It is not only in attention to persons, deputed by
Kings and Princes in Persia, that respect for royalty is shown ; it extends to the reception of letters,
dresses, and presents, and every inanimate thing
with which their name is associated.   The object
is to impart to all ranks a reverence and awe for
the sovereign and those to whom he delegates power.
In short, no means are neglected that can keep
alive, or impress more deeply, the duty of implicit
obedience.

Some time before we landed at Abusheher, the
Envoys of Scind had been at that port on their return from Teheran.   They carried, among other
presents to their Prince, a picture of his Majesty,

Fatteh Ali Shah. This painting was carefully packed in a deal-box; but the inclosed image of royalty could not be allowed to pass through his dominions without receiving marks of respect hardly short of those that would have been shown to the sovereign himself.

The Governor and inhabitants of Abusheher went a stage to meet it : they all made their obeisance at a respectful distance. On its entering the gates of the city a royal salute was fired; and when the Envoys who had charge of it embarked, the same ceremonies were repeated, and not a little offence was taken at the British Resident because he declined taking a part in this mummery.

CHAPTER VII.

NOTHING can be more striking than the change
from the Gurmaseer, or hot region, as they term
the arid track on the shores of the Persian Gulf,
to the fine climate and rich soil of the elevated
plains of the interior of that country. After travelling fifty-five miles, we reached the mountains.
From the village of Dalkhee, famous for its date
plantations, and streams impregnated with naphtha,
and which lies at the foot of the first range, we proceeded by narrow paths, which wound along the face
of the rugged and steep mountain we were ascending.
When near its summit, we were met by the Chiefs
of the tribes and villages in the vicinity. These,
with their principal adherents on horseback, were
drawn up on the crest of the mountain, while their

other followers sprang from rock to rock, firing
their matchlocks in honour of the strangers. Their
ragged clothing, their robust forms, their rapid
evolutions (which, though apparently in disorder,
were all by signal), amid precipices, where it
seemed dangerous to walk, the reports of their fire-
arms reverberating from the surrounding hills, gave
an interest to these scenes which a fine writer might
dwell on for pages, but I shall content myself with
the fact, that we passed in security the two great
ranges of mountains that intervene between the
sea-shore and the valley of Kazeroon; on entering
which, our eyes were not only cheered by rich
fields, but also with wild myrtle, blackberry bushes,
and willows. The latter, shadowing small but clear
rivulets, gave me and others a feeling of home,
which he who has not travelled in a far distant
land can never understand. Those of our party
who had not been in Persia before were quite
delighted at the change of scene, and began to give
us credit for the roses and nightingales which we
promised them on its still happier plains. What
they had seen of the inhabitants of the mountains
we had passed inclined them to believe the mar-

vellous tales we told of the tribe of Mama Sunee,
who boast of having preserved their name and
habits unaltered from the time of Alexander the
Great.

We had good reason, when on the first Mission,
to remember this tribe, who, in conformity to one
of their most ancient usages, had plundered a part
of our baggage that was unfortunately left without
a guard in the rear. The loss would have been
greater but for a curious incident. Among the
camels left behind was one loaded with bottles
containing nitric acid, which had been furnished in
considerable quantities to us at Bombay. The able
Physician * who discovered its virtues was solicitous
that its efficacy should have a fair trial in Persia;
and it certainly proved a sovereign remedy in an
extreme case, but one in which he had not anticipated its effects. The robbers, after plundering
several camel-loads, came to that with the nitric
acid. They cast it from the back of the animal
upon the ground. The bottles broke, and the
smoke and smell of their contents so alarmed the
ignorant and superstitious Mama Sunees, that they

* The late Dr. Helenus Scott.

fled in dismay, fully satisfied that a pent-up genie
of the Faringees had been let loose, and would
take ample vengeance on them for their misdeeds.
The truth of this was proved by the testimonies
of the camel-drivers, the subsequent confession of
some of the thieves, and the circumstance of several
of the loads which were near the nitric acid being
untouched.

The city of Kazeroon is situated near the ancient
Shapoor, with whose ruins antiquarians are delighted, and whose deserted fields were equally
prized by our sportsmen, from their abounding
with game.

I was myself much amused with a hunt of black
partridges* at this place, on which we were accompanied by thirty or forty horsemen. They scattered
themselves over a grassy plain, and the moment a partridge was flushed, the man nearest it gave a shout,

* The Derraj, or black partridge, takes its name from its breast,
which is of that colour; the rest of its body is very much variegated.
Its throat and legs are red, as also the under parts of its tail; its head
is black, arched with spotted brown and white feathers, and one spot
of white below its eye.

This beautiful bird is found in the higher latitudes of India and in
Persia; it is very common on the banks of the Tigris.

while such as were in the direction it flew rode after
the bird, which was hardly allowed to touch the
ground before it was raised again, and hunted as
before.   Its flights became shorter ; and after three
or four, when quite exhausted, it was picked up by
one of the horsemen, several of whom had little
dogs called " scenters," to aid them in finding the
partridge when it took shelter in the long grass or
bushes.   We caught about twenty brace of birds
the first morning that I partook in this sport.

Riza Kooli Khan, the Governor of Kazeroon,
came to pay the Elchee a visit.   This old nobleman
had a silk band over his eye-sockets, having had
his eyes put out during the late contest between
the Zend and Kajir families for the throne of
Persia.   He began, soon after he was seated, to relate his misfortunes, and the tears actually came to
my eyes at the thoughts of the old man's sufferings,
when judge of my surprise to find it was to entertain, not to distress us, he was giving the narration,
and that, in spite of the revolting subject, I was
compelled to smile at a tale, which in any country
except Persia would have been deemed a subject
for a tragedy : but as poisons may by use become

aliment, so misfortunes, however dreadful, when
they are of daily occurrence, appear like common
events of life.   But it was the manner and feelings
of the narrator that, in this instance, gave the comic
effect to the tragedy of which he was the hero.

"I had been too active a partizan," said Riza
Kooli Khan, "of the Kajir family, to expect much
mercy when I fell into the hands of the rascally
tribe of Zend.   I looked for death, and was rather
surprised at the lenity which only condemned me
to lose my eyes.   A stout fellow of a ferash *
came as executioner of the sentence; he had in his
hand a large blunt knife, which he meant to make
his instrument: I offered him twenty tomans if he
would use a penknife I showed him.   He refused
in the most brutal manner, called me a merciless
villain, asserting that I had slain his brother, and
that he had solicited the present office to gratify
his revenge, adding, his only regret was not being
allowed to put me to death.

"Seeing," continued Riza Kooli, "that I had no

---

* Ferash is a menial servant employed in a house to keep it clean
and take care of the furniture.   He also pitches tents, spreads carpets, &c. &c.

tenderness to look for from this fellow, I pretended
submission, and laid myself on my back ; he seemed
quite pleased, tucked up his sleeves, brandished his
knife, and very composedly put one knee on my
chest, and was proceeding to his butchering work, as
if I had been a stupid innocent lamb, that was quite
content to let him do what he chose.   Observing
him, from this impression, off his guard, I raised
one of my feet, and planting it on the pit of his
stomach, sent him heels over head in a way that
would have made you laugh (imitating with his
foot the action he described, and laughing heartily
himself at the recollection of it).   I sprung up ; so
did my enemy ; we had a short tussle—but he was
the stronger ; and having knocked me down, succeeded in taking out my eyes.

    " The pain at the moment," said the old Khan,
" was lessened by the warmth occasioned by the
struggle.   The wounds soon healed ; and when the
Kajirs obtained the undisputed sovereignty of Persia, I was rewarded for my suffering in their cause.
All my sons have been promoted, and I am Governor
of this town and province.   Here I am in affluence,
and enjoying a repose to which men who can see are

in this country perfect strangers.   If there is a deficiency of Revenue, or any real or alleged cause for which another Governor would be removed, beaten, or put to death, the king says, ' Never mind, it is poor blind Riza Kooli; let him alone :' so you observe, Elchee, that I have no reason to complain, being in fact better defended from misfortune, by the loss of my two eyes, than I could be by the possession of twenty of the clearest in Persia :" and he laughed again at this second joke.

Meerza Aga Meer, the Persian secretary, when commenting upon Riza Kooli Khan's story, said that his grounds of consolation were substantial; for that a stronger contrast could not exist between his condition, as he had described it, and that of others who were employed as Revenue officers under the present administration of Fars.   " I cannot better," said he, " illustrate this fact than by the witty and bold answer given a short time since by one of the Nobles to the Prince Regent at Shiraz.   The Prince asked of his advisers what punishment was great enough for a very heinous offender who was brought before him : ' Make him a Collector of Revenue,' said an old favourite Nobleman; ' there can be no crime for which such an appointment will not soon bring a very sufficient punishment.' "

We had an amusing account of an adventure which had occurred at Kazeroon to two Gentlemen of the Mission, who had been sent some months before to Shiraz. One of these, a relation of the Elchee, I have before mentioned as particularly averse to what he deemed unnecessary fatigue of body. But he and his companion had their curiosity so much raised by the accounts they received of two strange creatures, that were said to be in a house at the distance of fifteen miles, that in spite of the severity of the weather (for it was winter), and the difficulties of the road, they determined to go and see them.

In answer to their inquiries, one man said, " These creatures are very like birds, for they have feathers and two legs ; but then their head is bare and has a fleshy look, and one of them has a long black beard on its breast." But the chief point on which they dwelt was the singularity of their voice, which was altogether unlike that of any other bird they had ever heard of or seen. An old man, who had gone from Kazeroon to see them, declared it was a guttural sound very like Arabic, but confessed that

though he had listened with great attention, he had
not been able to make out one word they uttered.

When the party arrived, very fatigued, at the
end of their journey, the inhabitants of the small
village where the objects of curiosity were kept
came out to meet them. Being conducted to the
house where the birds were shut up, the door was
opened, and out marched—a turkey-cock and hen !
the former, rejoicing in his release from confinement,
immediately commenced his Arabic. The Persians
who came from Kazeroon were lost in astonishment,
while our two friends looked at each other with that
expression of countenance which indicates a doubt,
between an inclination to laugh or to be angry ;
the former feeling however prevailed. Their mer-
riment surprised the Persians, who, on being informed of its cause, seemed disappointed to hear that
the birds which appeared so strange to them were
very common both in India and England.

From the account given by the possessor of the
turkeys, it appeared that they had been saved from
the wreck of a vessel in the Gulf, and had gradually
come to the part of the interior where they then
were.

From Kazeroon to Dusht-e-Arjun is but a short
distance, but the ascent is great; and pleased as we
had been with Kazeroon, we found all nature with
a different aspect in this small but delightful valley,
which is encircled by mountains, down whose rugged
sides a hundred rills contribute their waters to form
the lake in its centre. The beauty of these streams,
some of which fall in a succession of cascades from
hills covered with vines; the lake itself, in whose clear
bosom is reflected the image of the mountains by
which it is overhung; the rich fields on its margin;
and the roses, hyacinths, and almost every species of
flower that grow in wild luxuriance on its borders,
made us gaze with admiration on this charming
scene; while the Persians, who enjoyed our looks
and expressions of delight, kept exclaiming, " Iran
hemeen ast !—Iran hemeen ast !" This is Persia!
—This is Persia !

I was rejoiced on this day's march to meet my
old friend Mahomed Riza Khan Byat, who had
come from Shiraz to compliment the Elchee. He
galloped up to me like a boy, calling out " You are
welcome." I could hardly believe my eyes on finding
him look younger and brisker than he did when I

left him ten years before, at the age of sixty-eight,
eating, every day, a quantity of opium that was
enough, according to the calculation of our doctor,
to poison thirty persons unaccustomed to that drug.
My regard for the old gentleman had led to my
taking no small pains to break him of a habit that
I was persuaded would destroy him ; and the doctor, from the same impression, was my zealous auxiliary. For him my friend inquired the moment he
had welcomed me ; when told he was in India, he
replied, laughing, " I am sorry he is not here; I
would show him that Christian doctors, though they
can, according to our belief, through the aid and
influence of their Messiah, work miracles, as he did,
by curing the blind and the lame, are not all true
prophets. He told me I should die if I did not
diminish my allowance of opium ; I have increased
it four-fold since he in his wisdom predicted my
demise, and here I am, near four-score, as young
and as active as any of them :" so saying, he pushed
his horse to speed, and turning his body quite round,
according to the habit of the ancient Parthians with
the bow, and the modern Persians with the match-
lock, fired a ball at a mark in the opposite direction

to that in which he was galloping. Riding up to
me, he first stroked his beard, which was too well
dyed to discover a single white hair, and then taking
out a box I had given him ten years before, opened
it, and literally cast down his throat a handful of
opium pills, repeating, " I wish my friend the
doctor had been here !"

I rode along with Mahomed Riza the remainder
of the march ; and, according to his account, the
condition of Persia was greatly improved.   Indeed
the internal peace it had enjoyed since the ·full
establishment of the power of the late king Aga
Mahomed Khan, must of itself have produced that
effect ; for Nature has been so bountiful to this
country in climate, soil, and in every animal and
vegetable production, that man, spoilt as he is by
her indulgence, cannot, without great and continued
efforts, destroy the blessings by which he is surrounded. I was more pleased at my friend dwelling
with a calm and contented mind on this great change
from a knowledge of his history. His father, Salah
Khan, was one of the chief Omrahs, or Nobles, at the
Court of Nadir Shah when that conqueror was murdered. On that event Kings started up in every

province.   Salah Khan among others entered the
lists.   He seized upon Shiraz, the fortifications of
which he extended and improved ; but his enjoyment of a royal name was short ; he was made prisoner, and put to death by Kerreem Khan.   His
son, whose character is marked by the absence of
ambition, has passed through life with respect as
the Chief of a tribe, but without enjoying, or perhaps desiring, any station of consequence.   He is
of a happy and contented frame of mind, and speaks
of the latter part of his father's life as a brilliant
but troubled dream of power, to which he was very
fortunate not to succeed.

The Prince and great men of Shiraz, on our
approaching that city, so loaded the Elchee with
presents of ice-creams, sweet-meats, preserves, and
delicious fruits, that all in camp, down to the keepers
of the dogs, were busied in devouring these luxuries.
A lion's share was always allotted to a party of the
17th dragoons, which forms part of the escort.   I
heard these fine fellows, who were all (with the exception of one man) from Ireland, discussing, as they
were eating their ices, their preserves, their grapes,
and nectarines, the merits of Persia.   " It is a jewel of

a country," says one. " It would be," said a second,
" if there were more Christians in it." " I don't so
much mind the Christians," observed his companion,
" if I could see a bog now and then, instead of these
eternal rocks and valleys, as they call them." " Fine
though it be," concluded corporal Corragan, " I
would not give a potato-garden in little Ireland for
a dozen of it, and all that it contains to boot." This
patriotic sentiment, which appeared to meet with
general concurrence, closed the discussion.

The morning we left Dusht-e-Arjun, I rode a
short way with an old reis or squire, who is a proprietor of a considerable part of the valley. " How
happy you are," I said, " in possessing a tract so
fertile, so beautiful, and with such rich verdure."
The old man shook his head : " That verdure you
so much admire," said he, " is our ruin ; our valley
is the best grazing land in Persia, and the consequence is, princes and nobles send their mules here
to fatten ; and while our fields of grain and our
gardens are trampled by these animals, we have to
endure the insolence, and often the oppression, of
their servants ; and these fellows in our country (I
don't know what they are in yours) are always ten
times worse than their masters."

CHAPTER VIII.

BEFORE I proceed further on my journey, I must
introduce my reader to some of the principal characters, Indian and Persian, with whom I associated. These were my companions every where;
and I owed much of the information and amusement I derived on my visit to Persia to their re-
marks and communications. No persons could
differ more from each other than my friends. This
resulted, in part, from their dispositions, but more
from the opposite scenes in which they had passed
their lives. But a short account of them will best
exhibit their respective characters.

The first, Mahomed Hoosein Khan, is a person
who is attached to the mission, more as a companion
to the Envoy, than in any specific employment.
He is my particular friend, and is one of almost

every party in which I mix; rides with me, talks nonsense with me, besides cutting jokes, writing epigrams, and telling stories; therefore I must give a short sketch of him, otherwise he will never be understood. Khan Sahib, or " my Lord," is the name by which my friend is usually known, though he has a right, from his inheritance, to the higher title of Nabob. He is about five feet three inches high; his face, though plain, has an expression which marks quickness and intelligence, and the lively turn of his mind has its effect heightened from an impression of gravity, conveyed by a pair of large spectacles, which, being short-sighted, he always wears. His frame is not robust, and his whole appearance indicates the over-care that has been bestowed upon his childhood, and the enervating pleasures in which his youth, according to the usage of Mahomedans of quality, has been passed. He has, however, notwithstanding early habits of luxury, if not of dissipation, received an excellent education. He is a tolerable Arabic scholar, and has few superiors in Persian; he writes that language with the greatest elegance, and is no mean composer, either in prose or verse. Add to these

qualifications a cheerful disposition, an excellent
memory, with a ready wit, and you have my little
friend.

The father of Khan Sahib was a Persian, who
went, in early life, to improve his fortunes in India.
He succeeded in recommending himself to Mr.
Duncan at Benares, and, after that gentleman became Governor of Bombay, he appointed his Persian friend Resident at Abusheher, and in 1798
sent him on a mission to the court of Persia. This
preferment naturally excited ambitious views ; and,
among other means by which he sought to ennoble
his family, was the marriage of his eldest son, my
friend, to the daughter of an ex-Prince of the
Zend family, who being in exile, and poor, was
glad that his falling star (to use an Asiatic figure)
should come in conjunction with one that he thought
was in the ascendant. But the father died soon
after he had grafted his son on this branch of a
decayed tree of royalty, leaving the latter what he
often laughingly calls, " The sad inheritance of
poverty and rank combined with a most dignified
wife," who, if he is to be believed, not unfrequently
reminds him of her high birth, and is rather wont

to dwell upon her condescension in allying herself to him. " I could," he added, the other day, " have given her some reasons for that act of prudence, but it would only have made her worse, and God knows what her violence might have prompted, so I kept quiet."

Here Khan Sahib betrayed his foible, which is certainly extreme prudence. He is in the habit of wearing yellow boots with high heels, loose red cloth trowsers, which are half displayed by a tunic tucked up, like that of the most valiant among the horsemen of Persia. His high lamb's-wool cap has, when he is equipped for a march, the true military pinch; two small pistols and a dagger are stuck in his girdle, and to a waistbelt is fastened a powder-flask and a bag of bullets; a large sabre hangs by an embroidered cross-belt, while a shorter sword, for close quarters, is fastened to his saddle; to the front of which is attached a pair of holsters that contain two large horse-pistols. In spite of all these indications of desperate courage, aided by an upright and imposing seat on horseback, and sufficient boldness in galloping to and fro on a smooth plain, there is some want of that forward

valour which depends more upon itself than the
arsenal of great and small arms it carries for its
defence. My friend is quite sensible of this deficiency, and is at times very happy in his allusions
to the fact, and can very wittily philosophise upon
the causes.—Want of stamina—coddled infancy—
indulged youth—fear of his father—and terror of
his royal wife, form the principal items in the list.
" But," he is wont to add, " if I have, from a combination of causes, lost that strength of nerve which
constitutes brute courage, I trust I have a manly
spirit, the result of reflection, which, on proper
occasions, you will always see me exert."

This is, no doubt, the case; but I never happened to be present on any of these " proper occasions," and I was one of a party, where we were
almost diverted from thinking of danger by his
ludicrous behaviour at its approach.

The Elchee having particular business when we
were lying in Abusheher Roads, had determined
to land ; though the sea was rough, and the waves
ran very high on the bar at the mouth of the
harbour. The Khan, who had recently been attached to the Mission, insisted on going, though

advised not : he was very courageous till we came
on the bar, where the waves that chased each other
seemed at every moment as if they would overwhelm
our little bark.   To each of these, as they rose and
pursued us with their foamy crests, Khan Sahib
addressed a rapid invocation—" Allah, Allah, Allah !" (God, God, God !) and the moment we were
safe from its fury, he, in a still more hurried way, repeated his gratitude ; " Shooker, shooker, shooker !"
(thanks, thanks, thanks !) These invocations and
thanksgivings were repeated with great volubility
and wonderful earnestness ; Allah, Allah, Allah !
and Shooker, shooker, shooker ! continued to sound
in our ears for a quarter of an hour ; when " Al
hamd ulillah !" (praise be to God !) pronounced
in a slow and composed tone, proclaimed we
were in smooth water.   I rallied my friend * on
the little composure he showed on this occasion ;
but he defended himself stoutly, saying, he always
prayed twice as much at sea as on shore.   This

---

* It is with great regret I state that the witty and accomplished
Khan Sahib, like many others mentioned in these pages, has paid the
debt of nature.   He continued in India as in Persia to accompany his
friend the Elchee till 1821, when he fell a victim to the cholera.

I believe; but he is on shore even an indifferent
observer of the rites of his religion, and is suspected
by some of the orthodox of our party of being a
Sooffee, or philosophical Deist, which seems to me
a general name, that includes all, from the saint
who raves about divine love, to the sinner who scoffs
at the rites of the worship of his country.

The next personage is Jaffier Ali Khan, brother
to the Nabob of Masulipatam. This Indian Mahomedan is a man high in rank though of limited
income, and has been from boyhood an intimate
friend of the Elchee. Having married into a
Persian family, he now resides at Shiraz, where
he has been for some time employed as an agent.
Jaffier Ali is a tolerable English scholar, but writes
that language with more facility than correctness.
He was, in his earlier years, extravagant from love
of dissipation, and is now imprudent from irresolu-
tion. He has acquired a good deal of knowledge,
but wants firmness of judgment. The consequence
is, that both in conducting his own affairs and
those of others, he becomes the dupe of rogues,
with whom such a character is sure always to be
surrounded. Nevertheless there is such a redeeming

simplicity of manner, and such kindness of heart, about poor Jaffier Ali, that it is impossible for any one to keep up that indignation which his folly often produces. " My friend is not the honest man I thought him," said he one day to me, speaking of a fellow who had duped him; " I have been more foolish than I could have believed, but I will take care another time: yet," he added, with a sympathy for his own weakness, " it is very difficult to deal with these Persians, they are so pleasing in their speech and manner, and most of all when they have cheating intentions."

Mahomed Hoosein, who is also an Indian, has served the Elchee as Moonshee, or instructor in the Persian language, since the latter was an ensign of eighteen, and has gradually risen with his master, whose confidence he enjoys and merits. He is a modest man, speaks little, but always to the purpose. It is not the habit of the Elchee to bring any man in his station prominently forward, and this practice appears exactly to suit the character of the Moonshee, which it has perhaps formed. He never goes to the Elchee but when he is sent for, and never stays when not wanted; is pleased with

any mark of flattering attention, but never appears,
like others, to make that his object. With this
happy temper, and an honesty that has stood the
test of great temptation for more than twenty years,
he passes a comparatively still life, amidst all the
bustle with which he is surrounded. When not
busy writing letters he is employed reading some
Persian book, chiefly works on the theological disputes between the Soonees and the Sheas. He
holds the tenets of the former; and, with all due
reverence to Ali, the nephew and son-in-law of the
Prophet, he thinks, with the Turks and Arabs, that
Abubeker, Omar, and Osman, were true men and
good Caliphs, and not as the Persians, in their enthusiasm for Ali, term them, base caitiffs and vile
usurpers. The Moonshee said to me one day, when
I was joking him on his studies, " I do not want to
dispute with these red-headed * doctors, but I must
fortify myself in my own belief;" and he added, in
a low tone of voice, " How can the faith of men be
right, whose practice is so wrong? Did you ever

---

* Kezzelbash, or red-headed, is the appellation by which the Persians are known over Asia. It is said to have arisen from their
wearing red cloth tops to their black lambs' wool caps.

see or hear such a set of swaggerers and story-
tellers ?   I rejoice my master has seen so much of
them ; he will think better than he has ever yet done
of us poor Indians."

The next person with whom I must make my
readers acquainted, is Meerza Aga Meer; he is a
Syed, that is one of the tribe of Mahomed, and
enjoys great respect among his countrymen, from
being a lineal descendant of a holy man, the Ameer
Hemza, whose tomb is at Shiraz, and is esteemed
one of the most sacred shrines of that city.   Aga
Meer is a fine penman, and an uncommonly good
writer of letters, which is his occupation.   He is of
mild and unassuming manners, slow in word and
action ; his even temper and good sense appear always directed to the object of keeping himself clear
of all taint from the scene of cupidity and intrigue
in which all around him are engaged.   The very
opposite of the generality of his countrymen, he
endeavours to shun all employment not in his own
line ; and, though a great favourite with the Elchee,
he takes nothing on himself, and will, indeed, do
nothing without a specific order.   Aga Meer is sometimes ashamed of his countrymen; but he is usually

satisfied with showing his feeling by a shrug of his
shoulders, and sometimes by averting his head, and
is evidently disinclined to inform against or condemn them, when he can avoid such a course without a breach of duty; but, whenever duty is in
question, this good and honest man is firm and
temperate in its fulfilment.

I have before mentioned Khojah Arratoon, the
Armenian treasurer. This sensible and honest man
has the characteristic reserve of his tribe, who, from
living in a country where they are subject to oppression, become, from early habit, most guarded
in their words and actions. This good man is fond
of a joke, but he whispers it to you as if it was a
state secret. We call him, as I have stated, Blue-
beard, from the circumstance of this dye being one
day predominant in the colour he had given to this
ornament of his face, of the size and form of which
he is, and not without reason, proud. He told me
his vanity was once not a little flattered by the
abuse of a Persian, who after exhausting all other
topics, concluded by saying, "And then what business has a dog of an unbeliever like you with such
a beard?"

The most prominent among the lower servants
is old Hajee Hoosein, the head of the personal attendants ; he assumes a superiority over his fellow-
servants on the ground of his having visited foreign countries ; and he boasts that from every one
of them he has brought away some advantage or
attainment. He has added to a taste for poetry
and the marvellous (which he tells me was born with
him in Persia) a love of antiquities, acquired at Bagdad—a knowledge of Arab horses, picked up at Bussorah—skill in traffic of small wares, learnt at Muscat—some theology, and the holy and useful name
of Hajee, or Pilgrim, gained by a visit to the Prophet's Tomb at Mecca; and a small but profitable
acquaintance with the machinery of clocks and
watches, obtained by a short apprenticeship with
an eminent horologist at Calcutta. This travelled
and very accomplished person, though he conde-
scends to hand the Elchee his Kellian, and to dis-
tribute coffee to visitors, is in great request throughout our camp, and with none more than me ; and I
am rather flattered by the partiality he shows for
my society, owing, I suspect, to my having early
declared my admiration of his various talents, and
in particular of his skill as a watchmaker, on his

having succeeded in making an old watch of mine, that had stopped for a twelvemonth, go for nearly one whole day.

The above personages are our principal characters; minor gentlemen will speak for themselves when they come upon the stage.

Besides these attached to our camp, we have numbers who, from frequent visits and dealings, are almost considered as belonging to it. But our mode of proceeding is now understood, and the Elchee is not compelled, as he was on his first mission, to guard against attempts of individuals to establish an exclusive influence. Two of these, made by very opposite characters, deserve to be recorded.

The first was a specious young man of some ability, whose name was Hajee Abd-ool-Hameed, who came from Shiraz with a complimentary letter from the minister, Cheragh Ali Khan, to whom he had promised to discover the real object of the Mission, while to others he had professed his intention of making himself the sole medium of communication and intercourse between the English Representative and the Persian Government.

He pursued his design with some address; but

the Elchee seeing him linger at Abusheher, and very assiduous in his court, suspected his motives, and one day plainly asked him, whether he had any further business, or entertained any expectations of employment? Though at first disconcerted by these direct queries, he confessed he had no business except that of recommending himself; and he then represented how impossible it would be to carry on any concerns in Persia without a qualified native as an agent, stating at the same time that he himself was exactly the man required.

The Elchee thanked him for his kind intentions, but informed him that such assistance was not at that moment necessary. If ever it was, he assured Abd-ool-Hameed, his disinterestedness, in coming so far to afford it, should not be forgotten. The manner more than the substance of this observation was death to the cherished hopes of the Persian expectant. Two days afterwards he left the camp and returned to Shiraz, where he became actively hostile to the Mission, considering himself, by a selfish but common perversion of human reasoning, not merely slighted, but robbed of all the benefits he had anticipated.

The rejection of this gentleman's services no doubt

prevented many speculators for favour making the
efforts they might have intended. But we learned
from Shiraz, that Aga Ibrahim, a native of Caz-
veen, who had been long settled as a merchant at
Shiraz, and was a candidate for the contract for
making up tents and other articles wanted for our
outfit, ridiculed Abd-ool-Hameed and his plan, and
boasted that he would show them all the way to
win a Faringee Elchee.

The intelligence of his intentions, which was
written by the Moonshee, Mahomed Hoosein, who
had been sent in advance with letters to the Prince
Regent of Fars and the King, made us anxious to
see this formidable personage. When we were a
stage from Desht-e-Arjun he made his appearance.
He seemed a merry open-hearted fellow, and, according to his own communications, fond of the good
things of this world. He was not over-scrupulous,
he said, as to a glass or two of good liquor, and he
boasted of having been a boon companion of the
King, when his Majesty was Prince Regent at
Shiraz, before dread of his uncle, Aga Mahomed
and the Moollahs, made him publicly renounce his
wicked ways, and march round the city to break
all the vessels which contained wine, in order that

young and old should be aware of the sincere repentance of the Heir Apparent of the throne of
Persia.

" I had no uncle with a crown on his head," said
Aga Ibrahim. " I care nothing for Priests, and
have never yet felt the slightest disposition to alter
my ways, except when the liquor was bad ; but I
take care," said he, with a significant nod to the
Elchee, " to have it always of the best."

This conversation occurred during the day. In
the evening, Aga Ibrahim desired a private interview with the Elchee, and after being some time
with him, he returned to our party evidently disappointed. We soon discovered the reason : he had
caused two loaded camels to be taken to the Elchee's
tent by a back road, and, after a short preamble,
had begged he would accept of both, with their burdens, as a " paish-kesh, or first-offering." One of
the camels was loaded with Russian brandy, and
the panniers which the other carried were (according to his report) two young and beautiful female
Georgian slaves! The liquor and the ladies had
both been politely declined, with many thanks for
his intended kindness.

Our friend, Aga Ibrahim, was a very different character from Abd-ool-Hameed. A few glasses of wine which we gave him restored his spirits. " My plan was a good one," he said, " and would, I thought, have won the heart of any Faringee. This Elchee must have some deep designs on Persia, or he could never have resisted such temptations."

Aga Ibrahim had been a great trafficker in the slaves, male and female, which the army of Aga Mahomed brought from Georgia in his irruption into that country in 1797. He had retained one in his own family, of whom he appeared dotingly fond. The more wine he took, the more he spoke of his favourite Mariamne. " I have often," said he, " offered to marry her, if she would only become a Mahomedan, but all in vain; and really, when she is on her knees praying before her cross, or chanting hymns to the Virgin Mary, she looks so beautiful, and sings so sweetly, that I have twenty times been tempted to turn Christian myself. Besides, I can hardly think of Paradise as delightful without Mariamne !"

Our jolly good-natured friend went back to

Shiraz next day with his camels, neither out of humour with us nor himself. He had failed, it was true, but he remained satisfied that it was some mysterious cause, against which human wisdom could not provide, that had defeated his excellent scheme for gaining the heart of a Faringee Elchee.

Aga Ibrahim was consoled for his first disappointment, by having a good share of the employment he desired, and, in all his dealings, he was found as honest as other Persian merchants.

CHAPTER IX.

WHEN we arrived at the garden of Shah Cherâgh, within a few miles of the city of Shiraz, a halt was ordered for the purpose of settling the forms of our reception. These were easily arranged, as the Elchee, though his military rank, from the period of his first mission to the present, had advanced from that of Captain to General, claimed only the same respect and attention he had before insisted upon as the representative of a great and powerful government.

Ceremonies and forms have, and merit, consideration in all countries, but particularly among Asiatic nations. With these the intercourse of private as well as public life is much regulated by their ob-

servance. From the spirit and decision of a public
Envoy upon such points, the Persians very generally form their opinion of the character of the
country he represents. This fact I had read in
books, and all I saw convinced me of its truth.
Fortunately the Elchee had resided at some of the
principal courts of India, whose usages are very
similar. He was, therefore, deeply versed in that
important science denominated " Kâida-e-nishest-
oo-berkhâst" (or the art of sitting and rising), in
which is included a knowledge of the forms and
manners of good society, and particularly those of
Asiatic kings and their courts.

He was quite aware, on his first arrival in Persia,
of the consequence of every step he took on such
delicate points ; he was, therefore, anxious to fight
all his battles regarding ceremonies before he came
near the footstool of royalty. We were consequently plagued, from the moment we landed at
Abusheher, till we reached Shiraz, with daily, almost hourly drilling, that we might be perfect in
our demeanour at all places, and under all circumstances. We were carefully instructed where to
ride in a procession, where to stand or sit within-

doors, when to rise from our seats, how far to advance to meet a visitor, and to what part of the
tent or house we were to follow him when he departed, if he was of sufficient rank to make us stir
a step.

The regulations of our risings and standings,
and movings and reseatings, were, however, of comparatively less importance than the time and manner
of smoking our Kelliâns and taking our coffee. It
is quite astonishing how much depends upon coffee
and tobacco in Persia. Men are gratified or offended, according to the mode in which these favourite refreshments are offered. You welcome a
visitor, or send him off, by the way in which you
call for a pipe or a cup of coffee. Then you mark,
in the most minute manner, every shade of attention and consideration, by the mode in which he is
treated. If he be above you, you present these refreshments yourself, and do not partake till commanded : if equal, you exchange pipes, and present
him with coffee, taking the next cup yourself: if a
little below you, and you wish to pay him attention,
you leave him to smoke his own pipe, but the servant gives him, according to your condescending

nod, the first cup of coffee : if much inferior, you keep your distance and maintain your rank, by taking the first cup of coffee yourself, and then directing the servant, by a wave of the hand, to help the guest.

When a visitor arrives, the coffee and pipe are called for to welcome him ; a second call for these articles announces that he may depart; but this part of the ceremony varies according to the relative rank or intimacy of the parties.

These matters may appear light to those with whom observances of this character are habits, not rules; but in this country they are of primary consideration, a man's importance with himself and with others depending on them.

From the hour the first mission reached Persia, servants, merchants, governors of towns, chiefs, and high public officers, presuming upon our ignorance, made constant attempts to trespass upon our dignity, and though repelled at all points, they continued their efforts, till a battle royal at Shiraz put the question to rest, by establishing our reputation, as to a just sense of our own pretensions, upon a basis which was never afterwards shaken.

But this memorable event merits a particular description.

The first mission arrived at Shiraz on the 13th of June, 1800. The King of Persia was at this time in Khorassan, and the province of Fars, of which Shiraz is the capital, was nominally ruled by one of his sons, called Hoosein Ali Meerzâ, a boy of twelve years of age. He was under the tuition of his mother, a clever woman, and a Minister called Cherâgh Ali Khan. With the latter redoubtable personage there had been many fights upon minor ceremonies, but all were merged in a consideration of those forms which were to be observed on our visit to the young Prince.

According to Persian usage, Hoosein Ali Meerza was seated on a Nemmed, or thick felt, which was laid on the carpet, and went half across the upper end of the room in which he received the Mission. Two slips of felt, lower by two or three inches than that of the Prince, extended down each side of the apartment.   On one of these sat the Ministers and Nobles of the petty Court, while the other was allotted to the Elchee and Suite; but according to a written "Destoor-ool-Amal," (or program) to which

a plan of the apartment was annexed, the Elchee
was not only to sit at the top of our slip, but his
right thigh was to rest on the Prince's Nemmed.

The Elchee, on entering this apartment, saluted
the Prince, and then walked up to his appointed
seat; but the master of the ceremonies * pointed
to one lower, and on seeing the Elchee took no notice of his signal, he interposed his person between
him and the place stated in the program. Here he
kept his position, fixed as a statue, and in his turn
paid no attention to the Elchee, who waved his hand
for him to go on one side. This was the crisis of
the battle. The Elchee looked to the Minister; but
he stood mute, with his hands crossed before his
body, looking down on the carpet. The young
Prince, who had hitherto been as silent and dignified as the others, now requested the Elchee to be
seated; which the latter, making a low bow to him,
and looking with no slight indignation at the Minister, complied with. Coffee and pipes were handed
round; but as soon as that ceremony was over, and
before the second course of refreshments were called
for, the Elchee requested the Prince to give him

* Ashkakas Bâshee.

leave to depart ; and, without waiting a reply, arose and retired.

The Minister seeing matters were wrong, and being repulsed in an advance he made to an explanation, sent Mahomed Shereef Khan, the Mehmandar, to speak to the Elchee; but he was told to return, and tell Cherâgh Ali Khan " That the British Representative would not wait at Shiraz to receive a second insult. Say to him," he added, " that regard for the King, who is absent from his dominions, prevented my showing disrespect to his son, who is a mere child ; I therefore seated myself for a moment ; but I have no such consideration for his Minister, who has shown himself alike ignorant of what is due to the honour of his sovereign and his country, by breaking his agreement with a foreign Envoy."

The Elchee mounted his horse, after delivering this message, which he did in a loud and indignant tone, and rode away apparently in a great rage. It was amusing to see the confusion to which his strong sense of the indignity put upon him threw those, who a moment before were pluming themselves on the clever manner by which they had compelled him to seat himself fully two feet lower on the carpet than he had bargained for. Meerzâs and Omrâhs came galloping one after another, praying different persons of his suite to try and pacify him. The latter shook their heads; but those who solicited them appeared to indulge hopes, till they heard the orders given for the immediate movement of the English camp. All was then dismay : message after message was brought deprecating the Elchee's wrath. He was accused of giving too much importance to a trifle; it was a mistake of my lord of the ceremonies; would his disgrace—his punishment —the bastinado—putting his eyes out—cutting off his head, satisfy or gratify the offended Elchee ?— To all such evasions and propositions the Envoy returned but one answer :—" Let Cherâgh Ali Khan write an acknowledgement that he has broken his agreement, and that he entreats my forgiveness ; if such a paper is brought me, I remain; if not, I march from Shiraz."

Every effort was tried in vain to alter this resolution, and the Minister, seeing no escape, at last gave way, and sent the required apology, adding, if ever it reached his Majesty's ear that the Elchee was offended, no punishment would be deemed too

severe for those who had ruffled his Excellency's
temper or hurt his feelings.

The reply was, the explanation was ample and
satisfactory, and that the Elchee would not for
worlds be the cause of injury to the meanest person
in Persia, much less to his dear friend Cherâgh
Ali Khan ; and a sentence was added to this letter
by particular desire of Meerzâ Aga Meer, who
penned it, stating, " That every thing disagreeable
was erased from the tablet of the Elchee's memory,
on which nothing was now written but the golden
letters of amity and concord."

The day after this affair was settled, the Minister paid the Elchee a long visit, and insisted upon
his going again to see the Prince.   We went—but
what a difference in our reception : all parties were
attentive ; the master of the ceremonies bent almost
to the ground ; and though the Elchee only desired
to take his appointed seat, that would neither satisfy
the Prince nor the Minister, who insisted that, instead of his placing one thigh on the Nemmed,
which was before unapproachable, he should sit
altogether on its edge   This was " miherbânee,
ser-afrâzee," (favour, exaltation) and we were all
favoured and exalted.

Such is the history of this battle of ceremony, which was the only one of any consequence there was occasion to fight in Persia; for in wars of this kind, as in other wars, if you once establish your fame for skill and courage, victory follows as a matter of course.

It must not be supposed from what has been stated, that the Persians are all grave formal persons. They are the most cheerful people in the world; and they delight in familiar conversation; and every sort of recreation appears, like that of children, increased by those occasional restraints to which their customs condemn them. They contrive every means to add to the pleasures of their social hours; and as far as society can be agreeable, divested of its chief ornament, females, it is to be met with in this country. Princes, chiefs, and officers of state, while they pride themselves, and with justice, on their superior manners, use their utmost efforts to make themselves pleasant companions. Poets, historians, astrologers, wits, and reciters of stories and fables, who have acquired eminence, are not only admitted into the first circles, but honoured. It is not uncommon to see a nobleman of high rank give precedence to a man of wit or of letters, who is expected to amuse or instruct the company; and the latter, confident in those acquirements to which he owes his distinction, shows, by his manner and observations, that usage has given him a right to the place he occupies.

I heard, before I mixed in it, very different accounts of Persian society. With one class of persons it was an infliction, to another a delight. I soon found that its enjoyment depended upon a certain preparation; and from the moment I landed in the country, I devoted a portion of my time to their most popular works in verse and prose. I made translations, not only of history and poetry, but of fables and tales, being satisfied that this occupation, while it improved me in the knowledge of the language, gave me a better idea of the manners and mode of thinking of this people than I could derive from any other source. Besides, it is a species of literature with which almost every man in Persia is acquainted; and allusions to works of fancy and fiction are so common in conversation, that you can never enjoy their society if ignorant of such familiar topics.

I have formerly alluded to the cause which leads all ranks in Persia to blend fables and apologues in their discourse, but this subject merits a more particular notice. There has been a serious and protracted discussion among the learned in Europe as to the original country of those tales which have delighted and continue to delight successive generations. One or two facts connected with this abstruse question are admitted by all.—First, that the said tales are not the native produce of our western clime. They are decidedly exotics, though we have improved upon the original stock by careful culture, by grafting, and other expedients, so as to render them more suited to the soil into which they have been transplanted.

The next admission is, that some of our best fables and tales came with the Sun from the East, that genial clime, where Nature pours forth her stores with so liberal a hand that she spoils by her indulgence those on whom she bestows her choicest gifts. In that favoured land the imagination of authors grows and flourishes, like their own evergreens, in unpruned luxuriance. This exuberance is condemned by the fastidious critics of the West.

As for myself, though an admirer of art, I like to
contemplate Nature in all her forms ; and it is amidst
her varied scenes that I have observed how much
man takes his shape and pursuits from the character
of the land in which he is born. Our admirable
and philosophic poet, after asserting the command
which the uncircumscribed soul, when it chooses to
exert itself, has over both the frigid and torrid zones,
beautifully and truly adds—

> " Not but the human fabric from its birth
> Imbibes a flavour of its parent earth ;
> As various tracts enforce a various toil,
> The manners speak the idiom of the soil."

The warmth of the climate of the East, the ever-
teeming abundance of the earth, while it fosters
lively imaginations and strong passions, disposes the
frame to the enjoyment of that luxurious ease which
is adverse to freedom. That noblest of all plants
which ever flourished on earth has, from the creation to the present day, been unknown in the East.
This being the case, the fathers of families, the
chiefs of tribes, and the sovereigns of kingdoms,
are, within their separate circles, alike despotic ;
their children, followers, and subjects are conse-

quently compelled to address these dreaded superiors in apologues, parables, fables, and tales, lest
the plain truth, spoken in plain language, should
offend; and the person who made a complaint or
offered advice should receive the bastinado, or have
his head struck off on the first impulse of passion,
and before his mighty master had time to reflect on
the reasonableness of such prompt punishment.

To avoid such unpleasant results, every bird
that flies, every beast that walks, and even fish that
swim, have received the gift of speech, and have
been made to represent kings, queens, ministers,
courtiers, soldiers, wise men, foolish men, old women,
and little children, in order, as a Persian author
says, " That the ear of authority may be safely
approached by the tongue of wisdom."

There is another reason why tales and fables
continue so popular in the East; we observe how
pleasing and useful they are as a medium of conveying instruction in childhood : a great proportion
of the men and women of the countries of which
we speak are, in point of general knowledge, but
children; and while they learn, through allegories
and apologues, interspersed with maxims, to appre-

ciate the merits of their superiors, the latter are, in their turn, taught by the same means lessons of humanity, generosity, and justice.

"Have you no laws," said I one day to Aga Meer, "but the Koran, and the traditions upon that volume?" "We have," said he, gravely, "the maxims of Sâdee." Were I to judge from my own observations, I should say, that these stories and maxims, which are known to all, from the king to the peasant, have fully as great an effect in restraining the arbitrary and unjust exercise of power as the laws of the Prophet.

It is through allegories and fables that we receive the earliest accounts we have of all nations, but particularly those of the Eastern hemisphere. We may, in these days in which exactness is so much valued, deplore this medium as liable to mislead; but must recollect, that if we had not their ancient records in this form we should have them in none. One of the wisest men in the West, Francis Bacon, has truly said, "Fiction gives to mankind what history denies, and in some measure satisfies the mind with shadows when it cannot enjoy the substance."

Those who rank highest amongst the Eastern nations for genius have employed their talents in works of fiction ; and they have added to the moral lessons they desired to convey so much of grace and ornament, that their volumes have found currency in every nation of the world.   The great influx of them into Europe may be dated from the crusades ; and if that quarter of the globe derived no other benefits from these holy wars, the enthusiastic admirers of such narrations may consider the tales of Boccaccio and similar works as sufficient to compensate all the blood and treasure expended in that memorable contest !

England has benefited largely from these tales of the East.   Amongst other boons from that land of imagination, we have the groundwork on which Shakspeare has founded his inimitable play of the Merchant of Venice.

The story of the Mahomedan and the Jew has been found in several books of Eastern Tales.   In one Persian version love is made to mix with avarice in the breast of the Israelite, who had cast the eye of desire upon the wife of the Mahomedan, and expected, when he came to exact his bond, the lady would make any sacrifice to save her husband.

At the close of this tale, when the parties come before the judge, the Jew puts forth his claim to the forfeited security of a pound of flesh. " How answerest thou?" said the judge, turning to the Mahomedan. " It is so," replied the latter; " the money is due by me, but I am unable to pay it." " Then," continued the judge, " since thou hast failed in payment, thou must give the pledge; go, bring a sharp knife." When that was brought, the judge turned to the Jew, and said, " Arise, and separate one pound of flesh from his body, so that there be not a grain more or less; for if there is, the governor shall be informed, and thou shalt be put to death." " I cannot," said the Jew, " cut off one pound exactly; there will be a little more or less." But the judge persisted that it should be the precise weight. On this the Jew said he would give up his claim and depart. This was not allowed, and the Jew being compelled to take his bond with all its hazards, or pay a fine for a vexatious prosecution, he preferred the latter, and returned home, a disappointed usurer.

Admitting that the inhabitants of Europe received these tales and apologues from the Saracens, the next question is, where did they get them?

Mahomed and his immediate successors, while they proscribed all such false and wicked lies and inventions, accuse the Persians of being the possessors and propagators of those delusive tales, which were, according to them, preferred by many of their followers to the Koran.   But in the course of time Caliphs became less rigid.   The taste for poetry and fiction revived, and Persian stories and Arabian tales deluged the land.

For some centuries the above countries were the supposed sources of this branch of literature, but, since the sacred language of the Hindus has become more generally known, the Persians are discovered to have been not only the plunderers of their real goods and chattels, but also of their works of imagination.   These we, in our ignorance, long believed to belong to the nations from whom we obtained them; but now that Orientalists abound, who are deeply read in Sanscrit, Prâcrit, Marhatta, Guzerattee, Canarese, Syamese, Chinese, Talingana, Tamil, and a hundred other languages, unknown to our ignorant ancestors, the said Persians and Arabians have been tried and convicted, not only of robbing the poor Hindus of their tales and

fables, but of an attempt to disguise their pla-
giarisms, by the alteration of names, and by introducing, in place of the gods and goddesses of
the Hindu Pantheon, the magi, and all the spirits
of the Heaven and the Earth, which peculiarly belong to the followers of Zoroaster.

Nothing, however, can impose upon the present
enlightened age, and our antiquaries have long been
and are still occupied in detecting thefts committed
twenty centuries ago. In spite of the Persian and
Arabian cloaks in which tales and fables have been
enveloped, the trace of their Hindu origin has been
discovered in the various customs and usages referred to, and it has been decided that almost all the
ancient tales are taken from the Hitôpadêsa, and
that still more famous work, the Pancha-Tantra,
or more properly the Panchôpâkhyân, or Five
Tales; while many of the more modern are stolen
from the Kathâ-Sarit-Sâgar, or Ocean of the Stream
of Narration, a well known work, which was com-
piled about the middle of the twelfth century,
by order of that equally well known Prince Sree
Hertha of Cashmere !

I have sometimes had doubts whether it was

quite fair to rake up the ashes of the long-departed
Pehlevee writers; more particularly as there does
not now exist one solitary book in their language
which we could compare with the Hindu MSS., of
which we have lately become enamoured; but reverence for the learning of those who have decided
this question, and dread of their hard words, with
the very spelling of which I am always puzzled,
has kept me silent. As I am, however, rather
partial to my Persian friends, I must vindicate
them from this general charge of robbery and
fraud. They certainly acquired one of their most
celebrated works of imagination from India, under
circumstances that do equal honour to the just king
Noosheerwân, his wise minister Boozoorchimihr,
and the learned doctor Barzooyeh.

The work to which I refer is the Kartaka-Dam-
naka of the Brahmins, the Kalîla-wa-Damna of the
Arabians, and the Fables of Pilpay of Europe.
This book, originally written in the Sanscrit, was
first translated into Pehlevee, from that into Arabic,
and next into Persian. So many learned Oriental
critics, French and English, have given the names
and dates of the translations, that I shall not re-

peat them, but give a short account of the first introduction of these famous fables into Persia, with
some facts of the life and opinions of the wise and
disinterested man through whose efforts his native
country became possessed of this treasure.

Noosheerwân, deservedly styled the Just, who governed Persia in the beginning of the seventh century, hearing of the fame of a work which a Brahmin of Ceylon had composed, employed the celebrated physician named Barzooyeh to obtain for
him a copy of this production. This was a delicate
and hazardous enterprise, for the work, ever since
the reign of a certain Indian King, named Dab-
shileem, for whom it was written, had been guarded
with great care and jealousy, lest the profane should
learn the wisdom that ought only to appertain to the
wise and holy.

Barzooyeh, confident in knowledge and strong in
allegiance, undertook to fulfil the commands of his
sovereign. He proceeded towards India, furnished
with money and every thing that could forward the
objects of his journey. When he arrived at the
Indian capital, he pretended that the motive which
induced him to visit it was the improvement of his

mind, by communication with the wise men for which it was at that period renowned. Amongst those whose society he courted, he early discovered one Brahmin, who appeared to him the very model of wisdom. His efforts were directed to gain his friendship, and believing he had succeeded, he resolved to intrust him with his real design.

" I have a secret to confide to you," said he, one day to his friend; " and you know, ' a sign to the wise is enough.'" " I know what you mean," said the penetrating Brahmin, " without your sign ; you came to rob us of our knowledge, that you might with it enrich Persia. Your purpose is deceit ; but you have conducted yourself with such consummate address and ability that I cannot help entertaining a regard for you. I have," continued the Indian, "observed in you the eight qualities which must combine to form a perfect man : forbearance, self-knowledge, true allegiance, judgment in placing confidence, secrecy, power to obtain respect at court, self-command, and a reserve, both as to speech in general society and intermeddling with the affairs of others. Now you have those qualities, and though your object in seeking my friendship is not pure

but interested, nevertheless I have such an esteem
for you that I will incur all hazards to forward
your object of stealing our wisdom."

The Brahmin obtained the far-sought book, and
by his aid and connivance a copy was soon completed.
Noosheerwân, who had been informed of the success of his literary envoy, was impatient for his
return; and when he arrived at the frontier, he was
met by some of the most favoured courtiers sent by
the monarch to conduct him to the capital. He
was welcomed with joy, particularly by Noosheerwân; a great court was held, at which all who
were dignified or learned in the kingdom were present. Barzooyeh was commanded to read from the
volume he had brought: he did so; and the admiration of its contents was universal.

"Open my treasury!" said the grateful Noosheer-
wan; "and let the man who has conferred such a
benefit on his country enter, and take what he finds
most valuable." "I desire neither jewels nor precious metals," said Barzooyeh; "I have laboured
not for them but for the favour of my Sovereign; and
that I have succeeded is rather to be referred to his
auspices, than to my humble efforts. But I have,"

said he, " a request to make : the King has directed
his able minister, Boozoorchimihr, to translate this
work into Pehlevee ; let him be further instructed
that mention be made of me in some part of the
book, and that he particularly specify my family,
my profession, and my faith. Let all this be written,
so that my name may go down to future ages, and
the fame of my Sovereign be spread throughout the
world."

The King was delighted with this further proof
of the elevated mind of Barzooyeh ; all present applauded his perfect wisdom, and joined in supplicating that his request might be granted.

Noosheerwân, addressing the assembly, said—
" You have witnessed the noble disinterestedness of
this man, you know how faithfully he has discharged
his duty, and what difficulties and dangers he has
encountered and overcome in my service. I desired
to enrich him with jewels and money, but such re-
wards have no value in his mind, his generous heart
is above them ; he has only asked that his name
shall have a separate mention, and that his life up
to this date shall be faithfully written. Let it,"
said the Monarch, turning to Boozoorchimihr,

" have a place at the very commencement of that
book of wisdom which he has procured for his
country."

The above is the substance of the story, as given
in the Persian translation of this work, made by
Aboo'l-Fazl, and called Eiyâr-e-Dânish, or the
Touchstone of Wisdom; and we have in the same
volume some particulars of the religious tenets, or
rather doubts, of the philosophic Barzooyeh, which
merit a short mention.

The wise doctor, who is made to speak in his
own person, expresses himself to this effect :—" The
questions regarding the attributes of the Creator,
and the nature of futurity, have been sources of
never-ending doubt and discussion. Every one
deems his own opinions regarding these important
subjects as the only true ones, and his life is wasted
in efforts to raise his own sect and to disparage
others ; but how many of these persons are mere
self-worshippers, in whom there is not a trace of
real religion, or of the knowledge of God ?

" How deeply do I regret that time which I
myself lost in pursuit of these vain imaginations,
searching every path, but never finding the true

way, and never even discovering a guide, I have
consulted the wise and learned of all religions as to
the origin of that faith in which they believed ; but
I have found them only busied with propping up
their own notions, and trying to overset those of
others.

"At last finding no medicine for the sickness of
my heart, and no balm for the wounds of my soul,
I came to a conclusion, that the foundation of all
these sects was self-conceit. I had heard nothing
that a wise man could approve; and I thought that
if I gave my faith to their creed, I should be as
foolish as the poor thief who, by an unmeaning
word, was deluded to his destruction.

"Some thieves mounted to the top of a rich man's
house ; but he, hearing their footsteps, and guessing
their object, waked his wife, to whom he whispered
what had occurred. 'I shall feign sleep,' said he
to her; 'do you pretend to awake me, and commence a conversation, in a tone loud enough to be
heard by the thieves. Demand of me with great
earnestness how I amassed my wealth; and, notwithstanding my refusal, urge me to a confession.'

"The woman did as she was desired, but the

husband replied, ' Do forbear such questions; perhaps if I give you true answers somebody may hear, and I may be exposed to disagreeable consequences.'

" This denial to gratify her curiosity only made the lady more earnestly repeat her interrogatories. Apparently wearied with her importunities, the husband said, ' If I comply with your wishes, it will be contrary to the maxim of the wise, who have said ' Never tell a secret to a woman.' '

" ' Who,' said the irritated lady, ' do you take me for; am not I the cherished wife of your bosom?' ' Well, well,' said the man, ' be patient, for God's sake; as you are my true and confidential friend, I suppose I must tell you all; but never reveal to any one what you shall now hear.' She made a thousand protestations that his secret should never pass her lips. The husband appearing quite satisfied, proceeded to state as follows :

" ' Learn, my dear wife, that all my wealth is plunder. I was possessed of a mysterious charm, by which, when standing on moonlight nights near the walls of the houses of the rich, I could, by repeating the word Sholim, Sholim, Sholim, seven times, and at the same time laying my hand on a moonbeam, vault on the terrace; when there, I again exclaimed, Sholim, Sholim, Sholim, seven times, and with the utmost ease jumped down into the house; and again pronouncing Sholim, Sholim, Sholim, seven times, all the riches in the house were brought to my view. I took what I liked best, and for the last time calling out Sholim, Sholim, Sholim, I sprung through the window with my booty; and through the blessing of this charm, I was not only invisible, but preserved from even the suspicion of guilt.

" ' This is the mode in which I have accumulated that great wealth with which you are surrounded. But beware and reveal not this secret; let no mortal know it, or the consequences may be fatal to us all.'

" The robbers, who had anxiously listened to this conversation, treasured up with delight the magic words. Some time afterwards the leader of the band, believing all in the house asleep, and having got upon the window, called out, Sholim, Sholim, Sholim, seven times, and springing forward fell headlong into the room. The master of the

dwelling, who was awake, expecting this result, instantly seized the fellow, and began to soften * his
shoulders with a cudgel, saying, ' Have I all my
life been plaguing mankind in acquiring wealth
just to enable a fellow like you to tie it up in a
bundle and carry it away; but now tell me who
you are?' The thief replied, ' I am that senseless
blockhead that a breath of yours has consigned to
dust. The proverb,' said the wretched man, ' is
completely verified in my fate ; ' I have spread my
carpet for prayer on the surface of the waters.' But
the measure of my misfortune is full ; I have only
one request to make, that you now put a handful of
earth over me.'

" In fine," adds Barzooyeh, " I came to the conclusion, that if, without better proof than delusive
words, I were to follow any of the modes of faith
which I have described, my final condition would
be no better than that of the fool in this tale, who
trusted to Sholim, Sholim, Sholim.

" I said therefore to my soul, if I run once more
after these pursuits, a life would not be sufficient ;
my end approaches, and if I continue in the maze of

* This is a literal translation.

worldly concerns I shall lose that opportunity I now
possess, and be unprepared for the great journey
which awaits me.

" As my desire was righteous, and my search
after truth honest, my mind was favoured with the
conviction that it was better to devote myself to
those actions which all faiths approve, and which
all who are wise and good applaud.

" By the blessing of God, after I was released
from such a state of distraction, I commenced my
efforts; I endeavoured to the utmost of my power
to do good, and to cease from causing pain to animals, or injury to men."

The wise physician adds in this passage a list of
all the virtues after which he sought, and all the
vices he shunned. This list is long, and appears
to me to include the whole catalogue of human virtues and vices. Suffice it here to say, that his bio-
grapher assures us that his latter end was blessed,
and that he left behind him a name as celebrated
for virtue as it was for wisdom.

CHAPTER X.

THE preceding chapter concluded with an epi-
sode upon the life and opinions of the favoured
physician of Noosheerwân. I must in this return
to my subject, the elucidation of the rise and progress of apologues and fables.

It will be admitted by all, that the Persians, in
the luxuriance of their imaginations, have embel-
lished wonderfully the less artificial writings of the
Hindus. The lowest animal they introduce into a
fable speaks a language which would do honour to
a king. All nature contributes to adorn the metaphorical sentence ; but their perfection in that part
of composition called the Ibâret-e-Rengeen, or Florid
Style, can only be shown by example, and for that
purpose I have made a literal translation of the

fable of the " Two Cats ;" from which I suspect
we have borrowed ours, of the " Town and Country Mouse."

" In former days there was an old woman, who
lived in a hut more confined than the minds of the
ignorant, and more dark than the tombs of misers.
Her companion was a cat, from the mirror of whose
imagination the appearance of bread had never been
reflected, nor had she from friends or strangers ever
heard its name.   It was enough that she now and
then scented a mouse, or observed the print of its
feet on the floor ; when, blessed by favouring stars,
or benignant fortune, one fell into her claws,

' She became like a beggar who discovers a treasure of gold ;
  Her cheeks glowed with rapture, and past grief was consumed by
    present joy *.'

This feast would last for a week or more ; and while
enjoying it she was wont to exclaim—

' Am I, O God ! when I contemplate this, in a dream or awake ?
  Am I to experience such prosperity after such adversity ?'

" But as the dwelling of the old woman was in
general the mansion of famine to this cat, she was

---

* This, with some other verses in the fable, are from Persian poets
of celebrity, whose stanzas it is an invariable usage to introduce in
such compositions.

always complaining, and forming extravagant and
fanciful schemes.   One day, when reduced to extreme weakness, she with much exertion reached
the top of the hut ; when there, she observed a cat
stalking on the wall of a neighbour's house, which,
like a fierce tiger, advanced with measured steps,
and was so loaded with flesh that she could hardly
raise her feet.   The old woman's friend was amazed
to see one of her own species so fat and sleek, and
broke out into the following exclamation :

> ' Your stately strides have brought you here at last ; pray tell me
>   from whence you come ?
> From whence have you arrived with so lovely an appearance ?
> You look as if from the banquet of the Khan of Khatâi.
> Where have you acquired such a comeliness ? and how came you
>   by that glorious strength ?'

The other answered, ' I am the Sultan's crum-
eater.   Each morning, when they spread the con-
vivial table, I attend at the palace, and there exhibit my address and courage.   From among the
rich meats and wheat-cakes I cull a few choice mor-
sels; I then retire and pass my time till next day
in delightful indolence.'

"The old dame's cat requested to know what rich
meat was, and what taste wheat-cakes had ?   ' As

for me,' she added, in a melancholy tone, 'during my life, I have neither eat nor seen any thing but the old woman's gruel and the flesh of mice.' The other smiling said, ' This accounts for the difficulty I find in distinguishing you from a spider. Your shape and stature is such as must make the whole generation of cats blush; and we must ever feel ashamed while you carry so miserable an appearance abroad.

> ' You certainly have the ears and tail of a cat,
> But in other respects you are a complete spider.'

Were you to see the Sultan's palace, and to smell his delicious viands, most undoubtedly those withered bones would be restored; you would receive new life; you would come from behind the curtain of invisibility into the plain of observation :

> ' When the perfume of his beloved passes over the tomb of a lover,
> Is it wonderful that his putrid bones should be re-animated ?'

" The old woman's cat addressed the other in the most supplicating manner : ' Oh, my sister !' she exclaimed, ' have I not the sacred claims of a neighbour upon you; are we not linked in the ties of kindred ? what prevents your giving a proof of friendship, by taking me with you when next you visit the palace ? Perhaps from your favour plenty

may flow to me, and from your patronage I may
attain dignity and honour.

> ' Withdraw not from the friendship of the honourable;
> Abandon not the support of the elect.'

" The heart of the sultan's crum-eater was melted
by this pathetic address; she promised her new
friend should accompany her on the next visit to the
palace.   The latter overjoyed went down immediately from the terrace, and communicated every
particular to the old woman, who addressed her
with the following counsel :

" ' Be not deceived, my dearest friend, with the
worldly language you have listened to; abandon
not your corner of content, for the cup of the covetous is only to be filled by the dust of the grave;
and the eye of cupidity and hope can only be closed
by the needle of mortality and the thread of fate.

> ' It is content that makes men rich;
> Mark this, ye avaricious, who traverse the world :
> He neither knows nor pays adoration to his God,
> Who is dissatisfied with his condition and fortune.'

But the expected feast had taken such possession of
poor puss's imagination that the medicinal counsel
of the old woman was thrown away.

> ' The good advice of all the world is like wind in a cage,
> Or water in a sieve, when bestowed on the headstrong.'

" To conclude, next day, accompanied by her companion, the half-starved cat hobbled to the Sultan's palace. Before this unfortunate wretch came, as it is decreed that the covetous shall be disappointed, an extraordinary event had occurred, and, owing to her evil destiny, the water of disappointment was poured on the flame of her immature ambition. The case was this; a whole legion of cats had, the day before, surrounded the feast, and made so much noise, that they disturbed the guests, and in consequence the Sultan had ordered that some archers, armed with bows from Tartary, should, on this day, be concealed, and that whatever cat advanced into the field of valour, covered with the shield of audacity, should, on eating the first morsel, be overtaken with their arrows. The old dame's puss was not aware of this order. The moment the flavour of the viands reached her, she flew, like an eagle to the place of her prey.

" Scarcely had the weight of a mouthful been placed in the scale to balance her hunger, when a heart-dividing arrow pierced her breast.

' A stream of blood rushed from the wound.
  She fled, in dread of death, after having exclaimed,

Should I escape from this terrific archer,
I will be satisfied with my mouse and the miserable hut of my
    old mistress.
My soul rejects the honey if accompanied by the sting.
Content, with the most frugal fare, is preferable.' "

This fable is a fair specimen of the style of such
compositions; but it is in the deebâchehs, or introductions to letters or books, that " The fiery steed
of the two-tongued pen" (meaning a split reed) is
allowed to run wild amidst the rich pasture of the
verdant field of imagination.

A better proof of the latitude taken on such occasions cannot be given, than in the preamble to
the treaty concluded by the Elchee on his first
mission to Persia, of which the following is a literal
translation.

" After the voice is raised to the praise and glory
of the God of the world, and the brain is perfumed with the scent of the saints and prophets,
to whom be health and glory; whose rare perfections are perpetually chanted by birds * of melodious notes, furnished with two, three, and four
pairs of wings; and to the Highest, seated in the

---

* A metaphorical name for angels.

heavens, for whom good has been predestinated;
and the perfume mixed with musk, which scenteth
the celestial mansions of those that sing hymns in
the etherial sphere, and to the light of the flame of
the Most High, which gives radiant splendour to
the collected view of those who dwell in the hea-
venly regions; the clear meaning of the treaty,
which has been established on a solid basis, is fully
explained on this page; and as it is fixed as a
principle of law, that, in this world of existence
and trouble, in this universe of creation and concord, there is no action among those of mankind
which tends more to the perfection of the human
race, or to answer the end of their being and
existence, than that of cementing friendship, and
of establishing intercourse, communication, and
connexion betwixt each other. The image reflected
from the mirror of accomplishment is a tree fruitful
and abundant, and one that produces good both
now and hereafter. To illustrate the allusions that
it has been proper to make, and explain these metaphors, worthy of exposition at this happy period
of auspicious aspect, a treaty has been concluded
between the high in dignity, the exalted in station,

attended by fortune, of great and splendid power,
the greatest among the high viziers in whom confidence is placed, the faithful of the powerful government, the adorned with greatness, power, glory,
splendour, and fortune, Hajee Ibrahim Khan; on
being granted leave, and vested with authority
from the porte of the high king, whose court is
like that of Solomon; the asylum of the world; the
sign of the power of God; the jewel in the ring of
kings; the ornament in the cheek of eternal empire; the grace of the beauty of sovereignty and
royalty; the king of the universe, like Caherman;
the mansion of mercy and justice; the phœnix of
good fortune; the eminence of never-fading prosperity; the king powerful as Alexander, who has
no equal among the princes, exalted to majesty by
the Heavens on this globe; a shade from the shade
of the Most High; a Khoosroo, whose saddle is the
moon, and whose stirrup is the new moon; a prince
of great rank, before whom the sun is concealed.

*   *   *   *   *   *   *   *

And the high in dignity; the great and mighty in
power; the ornament of those acquainted with
manners ******; delegated from the sublime quar-

ter of the high in power seated on a throne; the
asylum of the world; the chief jewel in the crown
of royalty and sovereignty; the anchor of the vessel
of victory and fortune; the ship on the sea of glory
and empire; the blazing sun in the sky of greatness and glory; lord of the countries of England
and India; may God strengthen his territories, and
establish his glory and command upon the seas, in
the manner explained in his credentials! which are
sealed with the seal of the most powerful, and most
glorious, possessing fortune, the origin of rank, splendour, and nobility; the ornament of the world; the
accomplisher of the works of mankind; the Go-
vernor-General of India!"

This preamble is not less remarkable for its
flowery diction than for the art by which it saves
the dignity of the king of Persia from the appearance of treating with any one below the rank of a
monarch.   It is also curious to observe, that after
introducing the king of England, how skilfully he
is limited to an undisputed sovereignty of the seas,
that his power may not clash with that of the mighty
Khoosroo of the day, " whose saddle is the moon,
and whose stirrup is the new moon," in his dominion
over the earth !

Speaking on the above subjects to Aga Meer, I asked him if their monarchs were as much delighted with this hyperbolical style as the Meerzas or Secretaries. "Not at all," said he : "the late king, Aga Mahomed, who was remarkable for his hatred of ornament and show in every form, when his secretaries began with their flattering introductions, used to lose all temper, and exclaim, "To the contents, you scoundrel *." "Flowery introductions," said the Meer, "if he had lived long enough, would have gone out of fashion ; but the present king prides himself upon being a fine writer both in prose and verse, and the consequence is, as you see in the preamble of this treaty, a composition which I know was honoured by his particular approbation."

It is but justice to some of the most distinguished Persian authors to add, that there are many exceptions to this redundant style of composition. In the pages of their greatest poets, Firdousee, Nizâmee, Sâdee, and Anwerree, we meet with many passages as remarkable for the beauty and simplicity of the expression, as the truth and elevation of the senti-

---

* Be-mezmoon Badbakht.

ments ; and many of their historians have given us plain narrations of facts, unencumbered with those ornaments and metaphors which are so popular with the generality of their countrymen.

How simply and beautifully has Sâdee depicted the benefit of good society in the following well known apologue !

" One day as I was in the bath, a friend of mine put into my hand a piece of scented clay. I took it, and said to it, ' Art thou musk or ambergris, for I am charmed with thy perfume ?' It answered, ' I was a despicable piece of clay, but I was some time in the company of the rose ; the sweet quality of my companion was communicated to me, other-wise I should be only a bit of clay, as I appear to be.' "

And in another* he has given, with equal force and simplicity, the character of true affection :

" There was an affectionate and amiable youth who was betrothed to a beautiful girl. I have read, that as they were sailing in the great sea they fell together into a whirlpool : when a mariner went to

* Both these Apologues have been translated by Sir W. Jones.

the young man, that he might catch his hand, and
save him from perishing in that unhappy juncture,
he called aloud, and pointed to his mistress from
the midst of the waves : ' Leave me, and save my
beloved !' The whole world admired him for that
speech ; and when expiring, he was heard to say—
' Learn not the tale of love from that wretch who
forgets his beloved in the hour of danger.' "

We often meet with Persian letters written in a
style at once clear and nervous. Of these there
cannot be a better example than that addressed by
Nizâm-ool-Moolk, the predecessor of the present
Soobâh, or ruler of the Deccan, to Mahomed Shah,
the weak and luxurious Emperor of Delhi. This
letter, besides the merit of its style, possesses that
of conveying a just idea of what Mahomedans conceive to be the duties and pursuits of a good and
great monarch, a character which is with them invariably associated with that of a military conqueror.

The following extracts from this well known production are very literal :

" It is the duty of princes to see that the laws are
strictly obeyed ; that the honour of their subjects
be preserved inviolate ; that justice be rendered to

all men; and that loyal nobles and ancient pillars
of the state, whose claims to reward are established
and acknowledged, be distinguished according to
their merits.   It is their duty, too, to seek for pleasure in woods and deserts*; to labour unremittingly
in the chastisement of the seditious and refractory;
to watch over the rights and happiness of the lower
order of their subjects; to shun the society of the
mean, and to abstain from all prohibited practices,
to the end that none of their people may be able
to transgress against the precepts of religion or
morality.

" It is also the duty of princes to be constantly
employed in enlarging their dominions, and in en-
couraging and rewarding their soldiery; it being
in the seat of his saddle alone that a king can properly repose.   It was in conformity to this opinion
the ancestors† of your majesty established it as a

* Alluding to hunting and other field sports.

† The Princes of Tartary.   The country we term Tartary is by
the Asiatics called Tûrkistan.   We have given the name of a small
tribe of Moghuls to the whole region inhabited by that and other races,
in the same manner as the Oriental nations called Europe Faringastân,
or the country of the Franks, because they first became acquainted
with the people of France.

domestic rule, that their wives should be delivered on their saddle-cloths, although the moment of child-birth is of all others the one wherein convenience and comfort are most consulted. And they ordained that this usage should invariably be observed by their descendants, to the end that these might never forget the hardy and manly character of their pro-genitors, or give themselves up to the slothful and enervating luxury of palaces.

" It is not in the melodious notes of the musician, or the soft tones of the mimic singer, that true and delightful harmony consists; but it is in the clash of arms, the thunder of cannon, and in the piercing sound of the trumpet, which assembles together the ranks in the field of battle. It is not by decking out the charms of a favourite female that power and dominion are to be maintained, but by manfully wielding the sword; nor is it in celebrating the Hoolee* with base eunuchs, that men of real spirit are seen to sprinkle each other with red, but it is in the conflict of heroes with intrepid enemies.

* A remarkable festival held in India, to celebrate the commence-ment of the new year, in which they fling red powder at one another: it commences at the vernal equinox.

" It being solely with the view of correcting the errors of your Majesty's government, and of restoring its ancient splendour, that the meanest of your servants has been moved, by the warmth of his zeal and attachment, to impart his sentiments to your Majesty, he has made up his mind to the consequences of this well-meant freedom, and will cheerfully submit to his fate; being in the mean time, however, determined (God willing) to persevere in the design which he has formed, of endeavouring to re-establish the affairs of the empire by every means that may be consistent with his duty and with propriety."

The affecting death of Yezdijird, the last of the Kaiânian race of kings, affords a fair specimen of that plain and distinct style in which some of the best histories of Persia are written. It is as follows:

" When the inhabitants of Merv heard that Yezdijird had fled from Persia, and was within their territory, they were anxious to apprehend and destroy him. They accordingly addressed a letter to Tanjtâkh, the King of Tartary, stating, ' The King of Persia has fled from the Arabs and taken refuge with us; we are not inclined to be his ad-

herents, we are more favourably inclined towards
you, whose approach we desire, that we may be
freed from him, and place ourselves under your
protection.'

" As soon as Tanjtâkh received this letter he desired to gain possession of Merv, and marched with
a considerable army towards that city. Yezdijird,
hearing of his near approach, and of the force by
which he was accompanied, departed from the Câra-
vânserâi where he had alighted, at midnight, un-
attended and undetermined where to go. As he
walked straight forward, he saw a light on the side
of a stream, to which he directed his footsteps. He
found a miller engaged in the labours of his mill,
to whom he said, ' I am a man in desperate circumstances, and have an enemy whom I have every
reason to dread; afford me an asylum for this one
night; to-morrow I will give you what may make
you easy for life.' The miller replied, ' Enter that
mill, and remain there.' Yezdijird went into the
mill, and laying sorrow aside, went composedly to
sleep. When the miller's servants observed that
he was gone to rest, and entirely off his guard, they
armed themselves with clubs, and falling upon him

slew him. Having done this, they stripped the body of the gold and silver ornaments, the imperial robe, and the crown ; then taking the corpse by the feet, they dragged it along, and threw it into the mill-dam.

" Next day Tanjtâkh arrived at Merv, and the inhabitants sought Yezdijird in every direction. By chance the miller being met, was interrogated. He denied having any knowledge of him ; but one of his servants, who was dressed in a woollen garment, having come before them, they, discovering that he smelt strongly of perfume, tore open his garment, and found Yezdijird's imperial robe scented with ottar and other essences, hid in his bosom. They now examined all the other servants, and found that each had some article secreted about his person ; and after being put to the torture they confessed the whole transaction.

" Tanjtâkh immediately sent people to search the mill-dam for the body, which they soon found and laid before him. When he saw the corpse of the king he wept bitterly, and ordered it to be embalmed with spices and perfumes ; and he further directed, that after it was wrapt, according to the

usage of the Kaiânian monarchs, in a shroud, and
placed in a coffin, it should be sent to Persia to be
interred in the same place, and with the same ceremonies, as other sovereigns of the race of Kaiân.

"Tanjtâkh also commanded that the miller and
his servants should be put to death."

What has been said in this chapter, and the examples of the various styles with which my opinions
have been illustrated, will satisfy the reader that
the mine of Persian literature contains every substance, from the dazzling diamond to the useful gra-
nite, and that its materials may be employed with
equal success to build castles in the air or upon the
earth.   My prejudices are, I confess, in favour of
the former fabrics, which in the East are constructed
with a magnificence unknown to the graver spirits
of our Western hemisphere.

CHAPTER XI.

OUR only occupation at Shiraz was feasting,
visiting, and giving and receiving presents. The
cupidity of the Persians exceeded all bounds, and
ministers, courtiers, merchants, wits, and poets, were
running a race for the Elchee's favour, which was
often accompanied by a watch, a piece of chintz,
or of broad-cloth. Their conduct confirmed me in
a belief I had imbibed at Abusheher, that all the
Persians were crafty and rapacious rogues. I like
to decide quickly, it saves trouble ; and when once
decided, I am particularly averse to believe my
judgment is not infallible.

The Envoy had hired, as before noticed, for his
Persian secretary, a mild moderate man, who appeared to have both good sense and good principle :
but although some time had elapsed, and I had

watched him narrowly without discerning a flaw,
I attributed this to his art, and I therefore gave
little heed to his reasoning when he used to plead
for his countrymen, urging (as he often did), that,
from our being strangers, and from our reputation
for wealth, generosity, and inexperience, we were
naturally exposed to the attacks of the cunning and
designing, from whose conduct we drew general in-
ferences, which were not quite fair. " We are not
all so bad as you think us," the good Aga Meer used
to say, with a smile; " we have some redeeming
characters; these may be rare, but still they exist;
but that, you English will as yet hardly believe."
He used frequently to mention to me, as one, a relation of his own, the Shaikh-ool-Islâm, or Chief
Judge and Priest of Shiraz : " He was," he said,
" a person who combined sense and information
with piety and humility. He has never come,"
added he, " like these greedy nobles and hungry
poets, to prey upon the munificence of the Elchee;
and when the latter, hearing that his sight was
weak, sent him a pair of spectacles beautifully
mounted in silver, he returned them, requesting a
pair set in common tortoise-shell." Though I heard

the account of this paraded humility with a smile,
I was very happy to find we were to meet this
paragon of modest merit at a breakfast, to which
Mahomed Hoosein Khan, the son of the minister
Hajee Ibrahim, had invited the Envoy.

The party assembled at the garden of Sâdee, and
we were seated near a fountain close to the tomb of
the Persian moralist. There was some punctilio in
taking our places : but the Elchee, though a stickler
for rank with the temporal lords, insisted upon
giving the highest seat to the Shaikh-ool-Islâm, who
at last consented to take it, observing, the compliment, he felt, was not personal, but meant to his
situation as a minister of religion.   I sat near, and
listened attentively to his conversation, in the hope
of detecting the Persian, but was not successful.
" You must," he said to the Envoy, " believe me
to be void of rational curiosity, and a man who
affects humility, because I have not only never been
to pay my respects, but when you sent me these
costly and beautiful spectacles, I solicited a cheaper
and less showy pair.   In both instances, however,
I acted against my personal inclinations from an
imperative sense of duty.   My passion," said the

Shaikh, " is to hear the history, the manners, and
usages of foreign countries ; and where could I have
such an opportunity of gratifying my curiosity as
in your society ?   I was particularly pleased with
the silver spectacles; the glasses suited my eyes;
and others in my house besides myself," said he,
smiling, " thought they were very becoming.   But
I was forced in both cases to practise self-denial.
The poor have no shield between them and despotic
power, but persons in my condition ; and they naturally watch our conduct with great vigilance and
jealousy : had I, for my own gratification, visited
you, and displayed on my person the proofs of your
liberality, they would have thought their judge was
like others, and have lost some portion of their confidence in my best efforts to protect them.   Besides,
ministers and courtiers would have rejoiced in my
departure from those rigid rules, the observance of
which enables us expounders of the Koran to be
some check upon them.   These were my motives,"
concluded the Shaikh-ool-Islâm, " for a conduct
which must have seemed almost rude ; but you will
now understand it, and not condemn me."

The Envoy was evidently delighted with his new

friend, and their conversation was protracted for several hours. The Shaikh-ool-Islâm endeavoured to impress him with a favourable opinion of the law of which he was an organ, and illustrated his arguments with anecdotes of religious and learned men, of which I shall give those that struck me as the happiest.

The celebrated Aboo Yûsuph, he said, who was chief judge of Bagdad in the reign of the Caliph Hâdee, was a very remarkable instance of that humility which distinguishes true wisdom. His sense of his own deficiencies often led him to entertain doubts, where men of less knowledge and more presumption were decided. " It is related of this judge," said the Shaikh-ool-Islâm, " that on one occasion, after a very patient investigation of facts, he declared that his knowledge was not competent to decide upon the case before him." " Pray, do you expect," said a pert courtier, who heard this declaration, " that the caliph is to pay your ignorance ?" " I do not," was the mild reply ; " the caliph pays me, and well, for what I do know ; if he were to attempt to pay me for what I do not know, the treasures of his empire would not suffice."

The orthodox Shaikh spoke with more toleration
than I expected of the Soofees, who, from the
wild and visionary doctrines which they profess,
are in general held up by the Mahomedan priests
as objects of execration. " There were," he observed, " many good and most exemplary men in
cluded in this sect, merely because they were en-
thusiasts in religion. Besides," said the Shaikh,
" both our poets, Hâfiz and Sâdee, but particularly
the former, were Soofees; and what native of Shiraz
can pass a harsh sentence upon them? We must,"
he continued, " lament the errors of Soofees in consideration of their virtues; and even in their wildest
wanderings they convey the most important lessons
—for instance, how simply and beautifully has Abd-
ool-Kâdir of Ghilan impressed us with the love of
truth in a story of his childhood *."

After stating the vision which made him entreat
of his mother to allow him to go to Bagdad and
devote himself to God, he thus proceeds. " I informed her of what I had seen, and she wept: then
taking out eighty dinars, she told me that as I

* This story is given in the History of Persia, vol. ii. p. 405.

had a brother, half of that was all my inheritance ;
she made me swear, when she gave it me, never to
tell a lie, and afterwards bade me farewell, exclaiming, ' Go, my son, I consign thee to God ;
we shall not meet again till the day of judgment.'
I went on well," he adds, " till I came. near to
Hamadân, when our kâfillah was plundered by
sixty horsemen : one fellow asked me ' what I had
got ?' ' Forty dinars,' said I, ' are sewed under
my garments.' The fellow laughed, thinking, no
doubt, I was joking with him. ' What have you
got ?' said another; I gave him the same answer.
When they were dividing the spoil, I was called to
an eminence where the chief stood : ' What property have you got, my little fellow ?' said he. ' I
have told two of your people already," I replied
' I have forty dinars sewed up carefully in my
clothes !' He ordered them to be ript open, and
found my money.—' And how came you,' said
he, with surprise, ' to declare so openly, what has
been so carefully hidden ?' ' Because,' I replied,
' I will not be false to my mother, to whom I have
promised that I will never tell a lie.' ' Child,'
said the robber, ' hast thou such a sense of thy

duty to thy mother at thy years, and am I insensible, at my age, of the duty I owe to my God?
Give me thy hand, innocent boy,' he continued,
' that I may swear repentance upon it.' He did
so—his followers were all alike struck with the
scene. ' You have been our leader in guilt,' said
they to their chief, ' be the same in the path of
virtue;' and they instantly, at his order, made re-
stitution of their spoil, and vowed repentance on
my hand."

The Elchee, before this party separated, endeavoured to persuade the high priest to allow him the
pleasure of a more frequent intercourse; but his
kind invitations were declined in a manner and for
reasons which satisfied me I had at least met with
one good Persian.

While at Shiraz, we were entertained by the
prince, his ministers, and some of the principal inhabitants. A breakfast was given to the Elchee, at
a beautiful spot near the Hazâr Bâgh, or thousand
gardens, in the vicinity of Shiraz; and we were
surprised and delighted to find that we were to
enjoy this meal on a stack of roses. On this a
carpet was laid, and we sat cross-legged like the

natives. The stack, which was as large as a common one of hay in England, had been formed without much trouble from the heaps or cocks of rose-leaves, collected before they were sent into the city to be distilled. We were told our party was the first to which such a compliment had been paid. Whether this was the case or not, our mount of roses, added to the fine climate, verdant gardens, and clear rills, gave a character of singular luxuriance to this rural banquet.

We were at several evening parties. The dinner given by the minister, Mahomed Nebbee Khan, was the most magnificent. He has been in India; and some English usages, to please and accommodate us, were grafted on the Persian. We went at five o'clock in the evening, and were received in his state hall. In the court-yard, in front of the room in which we sat, were assembled rope-dancers, wrestlers, musicians, lions, bears, and monkeys, all of which exhibited their different feats till sunset; when, after being regaled with coffee, kelliâns, and sweetmeats, we were conducted to another apartment, where we found a dessert of fruit very elegantly laid out in the English style. After sitting

in this room for about an hour, we returned to the
state hall, which we had no sooner entered than the
fire-works commenced; and though the space where
they were exhibited was very confined, they were
the best I ever saw. The rockets were let off from
a frame which kept them together, and produced
a beautiful effect. There was another sort called
zembooreh or swivels, which made a report like a
twelve pounder, and added great spirit and effect
to this exhibition. After it was over we had a
most sumptuous repast of fine pelaws, &c. and iced
sherbets.

The day before we left Shiraz, Derveesh Seffer,
my old acquaintance, paid the Elchee a visit. This
remarkable man, who has charge of the shrines *
(including those of Sâdee and Hâfiz) near Shiraz,
is esteemed one of the best reciters of poetry and
tellers of tales in Persia; and there is no country
in the world where more value is placed upon such
talents; he who possesses them in an eminent degree is as certain of fortune and fame as the first
actors in Europe. Derveesh Seffer, who is honoured

* Tekkeyahs.

by the royal favour, has a very melodious voice,
over which he has such power as to be able to imi-
tate every sound, from that of the softest feminine
to the harshest masculine voice. The varied expression of his countenance is quite as astonishing
as his voice, and his action is remarkably graceful,
and always suited to his subject. His memory is
not only furnished with an infinite variety of stories,
but with all the poetry of his country : this enables
him to give interest and effect to the most meagre
tale, by apt quotations from the first authors of
Persia. Those told by persons like him usually
blend religious feeling with entertainment, and are
meant to recommend charity; but I cannot better
conclude this account of my friend the Derveesh
than by giving a tale which he recited to the Envoy, with a view no doubt of impressing him with
a belief that worldly success might be promoted by
munificence, in any shape, to shrines like those of
which he had charge.

The Derveesh having seated himself in a proper
position, commenced with a fine passage from the
poet Nizâmee in praise of those who, possessing the
talent of recitation, give currency and effect to the

noble thoughts of departed genius.   After a short
pause he began his tale.

" In a sequestered vale of the fruitful province
of Khorassan there lived a peasant called Abdúlla.
He had married a person in his own rank of life,
who, though very plain in her appearance, had received from her fond father the fine name of Zeebâ,
or the beautiful ; to which act of parental folly
the good woman owed the few seeds of vanity that
mixed in her homely character.   It was this feeling
that led her to name her two children Yûsuph and
Fatima, conceiving, no doubt, that the fortunate
name of the son of Yâcoob, the vizier of Far'oun,
and fascinator of Zûleikhâ*, would aid the boy in
his progress through life; while there could be no
doubt of her little girl receiving equal advantages
from being named after the daughter of the Prophet, and the wife of the renowned Ali.

" With all these family pretensions from high
names, no man's means could be more humble or
views more limited than those of Abdûlla ; but he
was content and happy : he was strong and healthy,

---

* The frail wife of Potiphar, according to the Mahomedans.

and laboured for the reis or squire, who owned the land on which his cottage stood—he had done so from youth, and had never left, nor ever desired to leave, his native valley. The wages of his labour were paid in grain and cloth, sufficient for the food and clothing of his family and himself; with money he was unacquainted except by name.

" It happened, however, one day, that the reis was so well pleased with Abdûlla's exertions that he made him a present of ten piastres. Abdûlla could hardly express his thanks, he was so surprised and overjoyed at this sudden influx of wealth. The moment he could get away from his daily labour he ran home to his wife :—' There, my Zeebâ,' said he, ' there are riches for you !' and he spread the money before her. The astonishment and delight of the good woman was little less than that of her husband, and the children were called to share in the joy of their parents. ' Well,' said Abdûlla, still looking at the money, ' the next thing to consider is what is to be done with this vast sum. The reis has given me to-morrow as a holiday, and I do think, my dear wife, if you approve, I will go to the

famous city of Meshed : I never saw it, but it is
not above six or seven fersekhs distant. I will
pay my devotions at the shrine of the holy Imâm
Mehdee, upon whom be God's blessing, and like
a good Mahomedan deposit there two piastres—
one-fifth of my wealth—and then I will go to the
great bazar, of which I have heard so much, and
purchase with the remainder every thing you, my
dear wife and children, can wish; tell me what you
would like best.'

" ' I will be moderate,' said Zeebâ ; ' I want nothing but a piece of handsome silk for a dress ; I
think it would be becoming ;' and as she said so,
all the associations to which her father had given
birth when he gave her a name, shot across her
mind. ' Bring me,' said the sturdy little Yûsuph,
' a nice horse and a sword.'   ' And me,' said his
sister, in a softer tone, ' an Indian handkerchief
and a pair of golden slippers.'   ' Every one of these
articles shall be here to-morrow evening,' said Abdûlla, as he kissed his happy family ; and early
next morning, taking a stout staff in his hand, he
commenced his journey towards Meshed.

" When Abdûlla approached the holy city his
attention was first attracted by the cluster of splendid domes and minarets, which encircled the tomb
of the holy Imâm Mehdee, whose roofs glittered
with gold. He gazed with wonder at a sight which
appeared to him more like those which the faithful
are promised in heaven, than any thing he ever expected to see on this earth. Passing through the
streets which led to such magnificent buildings, he
could look at nothing but them. When arrived at
the gate of the sacred shrine, he stopped for a moment in silent awe, and asked a venerable priest,
who was reading the Koran, if he might proceed,
explaining at the same time his object. ' Enter,
my brother,' said the old man ; ' bestow your alms,
and you shall be rewarded ; for one of the most
pious of the caliphs has said—' Prayer takes a man
half way to paradise ; fasting brings him to its
portals ; but these are only opened to him who is
charitable.' '

" Having deposited, like a good and pious Mussulman, the fifth * of his treasure on the shrine of

---

* The Mahomedan law only requires a small deduction on account

the holy Imâm, Abdûlla went to the great bazar; on entering which his senses were quite confounded by the novel sight of the pedestrian crowd hurrying to and fro; the richly-caparisoned horses, the splendid trains of the nobles, and the loaded camels and mules, which filled the space between rich shops, where every ware of Europe, India, China, Tartary, and Persia was displayed. He gazed with open mouth at every thing he saw, and felt for the first time what an ignorant and insignificant being he had hitherto been. Though pushed from side to side by those on foot, and often nearly run over by those on horseback, it was some time before he became aware of the dangers to which his wonder exposed him. These accidents however soon put him out of humour with the bustle he had at first so much admired, and determined him to finish his business and return to his quiet home.

" Entering a shop where there was a number of silks, such as he had seen worn by the family of the reis, he inquired for their finest pieces. The shop-

of charity from what is necessary for subsistence; but of all super-fluous wealth (and such Abdûlla deemed his ten piastres), true believers were expected to give one-fifth to the poor.

man looked at him, and observing from his dress
that he was from the country, concluded he was
one of those rich farmers, who, notwithstanding the
wealth they have acquired, maintain the plain habits
of the peasantry, to whom they have a pride in belonging. He, consequently, thought he had a good
customer; that is, a man who added to riches but
little knowledge of the article he desired to purchase. With this impression he tossed and tumbled
over every piece of silk in his shop. Abdúlla was
so bewildered by their beauty and variety, that it
was long before he could decide ; at last he fixed
upon one, which was purple with a rich embroidered
border. ' I will take this,' he said, wrapping it up,
and putting it under his arm ; ' What is the price ?'

" ' I shall only ask you, who are a new customer,'
said the man, ' two hundred piastres ; I should ask
any one else three or four hundred for so exquisite
a specimen of manufacture, but I wish to tempt you
back again, when you leave your beautiful lands in
the country to honour our busy town with your presence.' Abdúlla stared, replaced the silk, and repeated in amazement—' Two—hundred—piastres !
you must be mistaken ; do you mean such piastres

as these?' taking one out of the eight he had left
in his pocket, and holding it up to the gaze of
the astonished shopkeeper. 'Certainly I do,' said
the latter; 'and it is very cheap at that price.'
'Poor Zeebâ!' said Abdûlla, with a sigh, at the
thoughts of her disappointment. 'Poor who?' said
the silk-mercer. 'My wife,' said Abdûlla. 'What
have I to do with your wife?' said the man, whose
tone altered as his chance of sale diminished.
'Why,' said Abdûlla, 'I will tell you all: I have
worked hard for the reis of our village ever since
I was a boy; I never saw money till yesterday,
when he gave me ten piastres. I came to Meshed,
where I had never been before. I have given, like
a good Mussulman, a fifth of my wealth to the
Imâm Mehdee, the holy descendant of our blessed
Prophet, and with the eight remaining piastres I
intend to buy a piece of embroidered silk for my
good wife, a horse and sword for my little boy, and
an Indian handkerchief and a pair of golden slippers
for my darling daughter; and here you ask me
two hundred piastres for one piece of silk. How
am I to pay you, and with what money am I to buy
the other articles, tell me that?' said Abdûlla, in a

reproachful tone. ' Get out of my shop !' said the enraged vender of silks; ' here have I been wasting my valuable time, and rumpling my choicest goods, for a fool and a madman ! Go along to your Zeebâ and your booby children ; buy stale cakes and black sugar for them, and do not trouble me any more.' So saying, he thrust his new and valued customer out of the door.

" Abdûlla muttered to himself as he went away, ' No doubt this is a rascal, but there may be honest men in Meshed; I will try amongst the horse-dealers ; and having inquired where these were to be found, he hastened to get a handsome pony for Yûsuph. No sooner had he arrived at the horse market, and made his wishes known, than twenty were exhibited. As he was admiring one that pranced along delightfully, a friend, whom he had never seen before, whispered him to beware, that the animal though he went very well when heated was dead lame when cool. He had nearly made up his mind to purchase another, when the same man significantly pointed to the hand of the owner, which was one finger short, and then champing with his mouth and looking at the admired horse, gave Abdûlla to under-

stand that his beloved boy might incur some hazard
from such a purchase. The very thought alarmed
him; and he turned to his kind friend, and asked,
if he could not recommend a suitable animal? The
man said, his brother had one, which, if he could
be prevailed upon to part with, would just answer,
but he doubted whether he would sell him; yet
as his son, who used to ride this horse, was gone
to school, he thought he might. Abdûlla was all
gratitude, and begged him to exert his influence.
This was promised and done; and in a few minutes
a smart little grey horse, with head and tail in the
air, cantered up. The delighted peasant conceived
Yûsuph on his back, and in a hurry to realize his
vision, demanded the price. ' Any other person but
yourself,' said the man, ' should not have him for
one piastre less than two hundred; but as I trust
to make a friend as well as a bargain, I have persuaded my brother to take only one hundred and
fifty.' The astonished Abdûlla stept back—' Why
you horse-dealers,' said he, ' whom I thought were
such good men, are as bad as the silk-mercers!'
He then recapitulated to his friend the rise of his
present fortune, and all that had occurred since he

entered Meshed.   The man had hardly patience to
hear him to a close ; ' And have I,' said he, ' been
throwing away my friendship, and hazarding a
quarrel with my brethren, by an over-zealous honesty to please a fool of a bumpkin !   Get along to
your Zeebâ, and your Yûsuph, and your Fatima,
and buy for your young hopeful the sixteenth share
of a jack-ass ! the smallest portion of that animal is
more suited to your means and your mind, than a
hair of the tail of the fine horses you have presumed
to look at.'

" So saying, he went away in a rage, leaving
Abdûlla in perfect dismay.   He thought, however,
he might still succeed in obtaining some of the lesser
articles ; he however met with nothing but disappointment : the lowest priced sword was thirty
piastres, the golden slippers were twenty, and a
small Indian handkerchief was twelve, being four
piastres more than all he possessed.

Disgusted with the whole scene, the good man
turned his steps towards home.   As he was passing
through the suburbs he met a holy mendicant exclaiming, ' Charity, charity ! He that giveth to the
poor lendeth to the Lord ; and he that lendeth to

the Lord shall be repaid a hundred-fold.'   'What
is that you say?' said Abdûlla.   The beggar repeated his exclamation.   ' You are the only person
I can deal with,' said the good but simple peasant ;
' there are eight piastres—all I possess ; take them,
and use them in the name of the Almighty, but take
care that I am hereafter paid a hundred-fold, for
without it I shall never be able to gratify my dear
wife and children.'   And in the simplicity of his
heart he repeated to the mendicant all which had
occurred, that he might exactly understand the
situation in which he was placed.

" The holy man, scarcely able to suppress a smile
as he carefully folded up the eight piastres, bade
Abdûlla to be of good heart, and rely upon a sure
return.   He then left him, exclaiming as before,
' Charity, charity ! He that giveth to the poor
lendeth to the Lord, and he that lendeth to the
Lord shall be repaid a hundred-fold.'

" When Abdûlla came within sight of his cot-
tage, they all ran to meet him.   The breathless
Yûsuph was the first who reached his father :
' Where is my horse and my sword ?'   ' And my
Indian handkerchief and golden slippers ?' said

little Fatima, who had now come up. ' And my
silk vest ?' said Zeebâ, who was close behind her
daughter. ' But wealth has changed your disposition, my dear Abdûlla !' said the good woman;
' you have become grave, and no doubt,' she added
with a smile, ' so dignified, that you could not be
burdened, but have hired a servant to bring home
the horse and to carry the presents for your family.
Well, children, be patient; we shall see every thing
in a few minutes.'   Abdûlla shook his head, but
would not speak a word till he entered his dwelling.
He then seated himself on his coarse mat, and repeated all his adventures, every part of which was
heard with temper till his last act, that of giving
his piastres to the mendicant. Zeebâ, who had a
little more knowledge of the world than her husband, and whose mind was ruffled by disappointment, loudly reproached him with his stupidity and
folly in thus throwing away the money he had obtained by the liberality of the reis, to whom she
immediately went and gave information of all that
had occurred.   The enraged squire sent for Abdûlla: ' You blockhead,' said he, ' what have you
been about ? I, who am a man of substance,

never give more than a copper coin * to these va-
gabond rascals who go about asking charity; and
here you have given one of them eight piastres;
enough to spoil the whole generation: but he promised you a hundred-fold, and you shall have it to
prevent future folly. Here,' said he to the servants
near him, ' seize the fellow, and give him a hundred
stripes!' The order was obeyed as soon as given,
and poor Abdûlla went home on the night of the
day following that which had dawned upon his
wealth, sore from a beating, without a coin in his
pocket, out of temper with silk-mercers, horse-
dealers, cutlers, slipper-makers, mendicants, squires,
wives, himself, and all the world.

"Early next morning Abdûlla was awakened
by a message, that the reis wanted him. Before
he went he had forgiven his wife, who was much
grieved at the punishment which her indiscretion
had brought upon her husband. He also kissed
his children, and bid them be of good heart, for he
might yet, through God's favour, make amends for
the disappointment he had caused them. When

---

* " Pool-e-siyâh," literally, black coin.

he came to the reis, the latter said, ' I have found
a job for you, Abdûlla, that will bring you to your
senses: here, in this dry soil, I mean to dig for
water, and you must toil day after day till it is
found.' So saying, he went away, leaving Abdûlla
to his own sad reflections and hard labour. He
made little progress the first two days; but on the
third, when about six cubits below the surface, he
came upon a brass vessel: on looking into which
he found it full of round white stones, which were
beautiful from their smoothness and fine lustre.
He tried to break one with his teeth, but could not.
' Well,' said he, ' this is no doubt some of the rice
belonging to the squire which has been turned into
stones: I am glad of it—he is a cruel master; I
will however take them home—they are very pretty;
and now I recollect I saw some very like them at
Meshed for sale. But what can this be,' said Abdûlla to himself, disengaging another pot from the
earth—' Oho! these are darker, they must have
been wheat—but they are very beautiful; and
here!' cried he, ' these shining pieces of glass are
finer and brighter than all the rest; but I will try if

they are glass;' and he put one of them between
two stones, but could not break it.

" Pleased with this discovery, and believing he
had got something valuable, but ignorant what it
was, he dug out all he could find, and putting them
into a bag carefully concealed it even from his wife.
His plan was, to obtain a day's leave from his master, and go again to Meshed, where he had hopes
of selling the pretty stones of various colours for as
much money as would purchase the silk vest, the
horse, the sword, the slippers, and the handkerchief.
His mind dwelt with satisfaction on the pleasing
surprise it would be to those he loved, to see him
return home, mounted on the horse, and loaded
with the other articles.   But while the pious Abdûlla indulged in this dream, he always resolved
that the Imâm Mehdee should receive a fifth of
whatever wealth he obtained.

" After some weeks hard labour at the well water
was found.   The reis was in good humour, and
the boon of a holiday was granted.   Abdûlla departed before day-light, that no one might see the
bag which he carried; when close to Meshed, he

concealed it near the root of a tree, having first taken out two handfuls of the pretty stones, to try what kind of a market he could make of them. He went to a shop where he had seen some like them. He asked the man, pointing to those in the shop, if he would buy any such articles ? ' Certainly,' said the jeweller, for such he was ; ' have you one to sell ?' ' One !' said Abdûlla, ' I have plenty.' ' Plenty !' repeated the man. ' Yes ; a bag-full.' ' Common pebbles, I suppose ; can you show me any ?' ' Look here !' said Abdûlla, taking out a handful, which so surprised the jeweller that it was some time before he could speak. ' Will you remain here, honest man,' said he, ' for a moment,' trembling as he spoke, ' and I will return instantly.' So saying, he left the shop, but re-appeared in a few minutes with the chief magistrate and some of his attendants. ' There is the man,' said he ; ' I am innocent of all dealings with him : he has found the long lost treasure of Khoosroo*; his pockets are filled with diamonds, rubies, and pearls, in price and lustre far beyond any existing ; and he says he has a bag-full.' The magistrate ordered Abdûlla to be

---

* Cyrus. There is a common belief in Persia that an immense treasure was buried by this monarch.

searched, and the jewels which had been described
were found.   He was then desired to show where
he had deposited the bag, which he did; all were
carefully sealed, and carried with Abdûlla to the
governor, by whom he was strictly examined.   He
told his whole history from first to last: the receiving of ten piastres; his charity at the shrine of
the Imâm; his intended purchases; the conduct
of the mercer, the horse-dealer, the cutler, the slip-
per-maker; the promises of the mendicant; the
disappointment and anger of his wife; the cruelty
of the reis; the digging of the well; the discovery
of the pretty stones; the plan formed for disposing
of them, with the reserve for further charity: all
this was narrated with a clearness and simplicity
that stamped its truth, which was confirmed by the
testimony of his wife and children, who were brought
to Meshed.   But notwithstanding this, Abdûlla, his
family, and the treasures he had found, were a few
days afterwards despatched for Isfahan, under a
guard of five hundred horsemen.   Express couriers
were sent before to advise the ministers of the great
Abbas of the discovery which had been made, and
of all that had been done.

    " During these proceedings at Meshed, extra-

ordinary events occurred at Isfahan. Shah Abbas
the Great saw one night in a dream the holy Imâm
Mehdee, clothed in green robes. The saint, after
looking steadfastly at the monarch, exclaimed,
' Abbas, protect and favour my friend!' The
king was much troubled at this dream, and desired his astrologers and wise men to expound it:
but they could not. On the two following nights
the same vision appeared, and the same words
were pronounced. The monarch lost all temper,
and threatened the chief astrologer and others with
death, unless they relieved the anxiety of his mind
before the evening of the same day. While pre-
parations were making for their execution, the
couriers from the governor of Meshed arrived,
and the vizier, after perusing the letters, hastened
to the king. ' Let the mind of the refuge * of the
world be at repose,' he said ; ' for the dream of
our monarch is explained. The peasant Abdûlla
of Khorassan, who, though ignorant and poor, is
pious and charitable, and who has become the
chosen instrument of Providence for discovering

* Jehân-Penâh.

the treasures of Khoosroo, is the revealed friend of
the holy Imâm Mehdee, who has commanded that
this good and humble man be honoured by the
protection and favour of the king of kings.'

" Shah Abbas listened to the particulars which
were written from Meshed with delight ; his mind
was quite relieved, and he ordered all his nobles
and his army to accompany him a day's march
from Isfahan to meet the friend of the holy Imâm.
When the approach of the party was announced,
the king walked from his tent a short distance to
meet them.   First came one hundred horsemen ;
next Abdûlla, with his arms bound, sitting on a
camel ; after him, on another, his wife Zeebâ, and
followed by their children, Yûsuph and Fatima,
riding together on a third.   Behind the prisoners
was the treasure.   A hundred horsemen guarded
each flank, and two hundred covered the rear,
Shah Abbas made the camels which carried Abdûlla and his family kneel close to him, and aided,
with his royal hands, to untie the cords by which
the good man was bound, while others released his
wife and children.   A suit of the king's own robes
were directed to be put upon Abdûlla, and the

monarch led him to a seat close to his throne:
but before he would consent to be seated, he thus
addressed his majesty.

"' O King of the Universe, I am a poor man, but
I was contented with my lot, and happy in my family, till I first knew wealth. From that day my
life has been a series of misfortunes: folly and ambition have made me entertain wishes out of my
sphere, and I have brought disappointment and
misfortune on those I loved best; but now that
my death is near, and it pleases your majesty to
amuse yourself with a mock-honour to your slave,
he is satisfied, if your royal clemency will only spare
the lives of that kind woman and these dear children. Let them be restored to the peace and innocence of their native valley, and deal with me
according to your royal pleasure.'

" On uttering these words, Abdûlla, overcome by
his feelings, burst into tears. Abbas was himself
greatly moved. ' Good and pious man,' he said,
' I intend to honour, not to slay thee. Thy humble
and sincere prayers, and thy charitable offerings at
the shrine of the holy Mehdee, have been approved

and accepted. He has commanded me to protect
and favour thee. Thou shalt stay a few days at
my capital, to recover from thy fatigues, and return as governor of that province from which thou
hast come a prisoner. A wise minister, versed in
the forms of office, shall attend thee; but in thy
piety and honesty of character I shall find the best
qualities for him who is destined to rule over
others. Thy good wife Zeebâ has already received
the silk vest she so anxiously expected ; and it shall
be my charge,' continued the gracious monarch,
with a smile, ' to see Yûsuph provided with a
horse and sword, and that little Fatima shall have
her handkerchief and golden slippers.'

" The manner as well as the expressions of the
king dispelled all Abdûlla's fears, and filled his
heart with boundless gratitude. He was soon after
nominated governor of Khorassan, and became famous over the country for his humanity and justice.
He repaired, beautified, and richly endowed the
shrine of the holy Imâm, to whose guardian care
he ever ascribed his advancement. Yûsuph became a favourite of Abbas, and was distinguished

by his skill in horsemanship, and by his gallantry.
Fatima was married to one of the principal nobles,
and the good Zeebâ had the satisfaction through
life of being sole mistress in her family, and having
no rival in the affection of her husband, who continued to cherish, in his exalted situation, those
ties and feelings which had formed his happiness
in humble life."

Such is the story of Abdûlla of Khorassan, as
given by my friend Derveesh Seffer ; but the difference between perusing it and hearing him tell it, is
that between reading a play and seeing it acted by
the first performers.   I had heard him tell this tale
ten years before, when a curious incident occurred.
Two gentlemen rose to leave the party when he was
commencing : he asked the cause of their departure.
" They do not understand Persian," I said. " That
is of no consequence," he replied ; " entreat them
to stay, and they will soon find that their ignorance
of the language does not place them beyond my
power." His wishes were explained, and the result
proved he was correct : they were nearly as much
entertained as others, and had their feelings almost
equally excited ; such was his admirable expression

of countenance, and so varied the intonations of his voice.

I was pleased to see my friend Derveesh Seffer treated with liberality by the Elchee. Such conduct towards persons of his character and profession makes useful impressions. But here, as elsewhere, much depends upon the selection of proper objects of notice; and it is no easy matter to resist the constant attempts which are made to obtain money or presents.

A poet of Shiraz, named Moollâh Adam, had gone a stage from that city to present an ode to the Elchee, whom he had in this long and laboured production compared to Roostem, the hero of Persia, for valour ; to Peerân-Weeseh, the Solomon of Tartary, for wisdom ; and to Hâtim-Tâi, the most munificent of Arabian princes, for generosity. He had been rewarded for his trouble, but was not satisfied, and his genius was taxed to obtain something more. While we were sitting in the room, at the gateway of the beautiful garden of Jehân-Noomâ, looking at the mules carrying our baggage towards Isfahan, this votary of the muses made his appearance : his professed object was to take leave ; his real purpose was to read an epigram of four lines *, the concluding one of which was —

" Moollâh Adam neek sâ'et yâft."

This line, from sâ'et signifying hour or watch, might either be translated,

" Moollâh Adam chose a good (or propitious) hour."

or,

" Moollâh Adam got a good watch."

The animals, laden with the most valuable articles, were at the moment on the road below the window where we were seated, and the Elchee, pointing to them, said, " Sâ'et goozesht," the hour is past, or, the watch is gone. The countenance of the poet, which had, on reading his last line, glistened with expectation, changed for a moment, but was soon covered with forced smiles, and he declared that he would rather carry the Elchee's happy reply into the city than ten watches. I trembled lest this flattery should succeed : it did not ; and he departed apparently in good humour, but inwardly, no doubt, much disappointed.

* Roobâi or Quatrain.

CHAPTER XII.

THE formation of the Elchee's establishment, which had commenced at Abusheher, was completed at Shiraz. Servants of every description were hired; and in all cases the preference was given to those who had been on our first mission; when such were dead, that was transferred to their brothers, sons, or near relations.

The Persians are more than good-looking, they are a handsome race of men. All the public and private servants of the mission were dressed in silk or cloth tunics, with new lamb's-wool caps, many with silk and some with shawl-waistbands; besides, they were all clean, and had their beards well-trimmed for the occasion, knowing that, to those who pretend to figure in the train of an Elchee, personal appearance is of no slight consequence.

Thus attended, we proceeded towards the foot-stool of royalty. Nine splendidly dressed Jelloodârs or grooms, under the direction of a Meer-Akhoor, or - master-of-the-horse, led nine beautiful horses, richly caparisoned, with saddles and bridles finely ornamented with gold and silver. Next came eight Shâtirs, or running footmen, dressed in tunics of yellow cloth, trimmed with silver; and then the Elchee and suite, followed by a large escort of cavalry, with kettle-drums and trumpets. On the flanks of this state-line of march were all kinds of Meerzâs *, or secretaries, and attendants. Amongst the most essential of the latter were the Paish-Khid-mets, or personal servants, who prepared kelliâns or pipes for the Elchee and the gentlemen of his train. These were mounted, and carried before them, fixed like holsters, two large cases which contained their kelliâns, and all the implements thereunto appertaining. The most extraordinary part of their equipment was two small iron chafing-dishes filled with charcoal, which hung by chains, dangling below their stirrups. From these grates they lighted the

* The word Meerzâ, when prefixed to a name, implies a secretary or civilian ; when it follows, it designates a prince.

kelliân, which they held in their hands, presenting
their masters with the end of a long pliant tube,
through which the latter smoked, while the Paish-
Khidmets rode a few paces in the rear.

Our cavalcade always preserved the same order
even during our long night-marches, the tedious-
ness of which suggested that our party wanted a
minstrel to shorten the distance by tales of wonder.
This want was no sooner hinted, than an old groom,
called Joozee Beg, came forward and offered his services. He belonged, he said, to the Zend tribe,
and when its chiefs were kings of Persia he was
not neglected. " Moorâd Ali Khan, and Lootf Ali
Khan, that miracle of valour," said old Joozee Beg,
" have listened to my voice, when it was exerted to
animate* their followers to battle; but these days
are gone; a Turkish family wears the crown of
Iran†; I am, like others of my race, in indigence
and obscurity, and now recite verses, which princes
loved to hear, to men like myself of low degree;

* It has long been the custom in Persia for persons to recite ani-
mating verses, from the Shâh-Nâmeh, at the commencement of, and
during a battle. The late king, Aga Mahomed, was particularly fond
of this usage, and bestowed marks of his favour on such minstrels.

† Iran is the ancient name of Persia, as Turan is of Tartary.

but if the Elchee desires, I will repeat some lines
fit for a soldier to listen to, from the Shâh-Nâmeh
of Firdousee." This prelude gave more pleasure,
from its near resemblance to that of our well-known
northern minstrel:

> " No longer courted and caressed,
>   High placed in hall, a welcome guest,
>   He poured, to lord and lady gay,
>   The unpremeditated lay.—
>   Old times are past, old manners gone,
>   A stranger filled the Stuart's throne.
>   A wandering harper, scorned and poor,
>   He begged his bread from door to door,
>   And tuned, to please a peasant's ear,
>   The harp a king had loved to hear."

Joozee Beg was told his offer was accepted, and
after giving the horse he led to another, and taking
his place in the front of the running footmen, he
began as follows.

" It is hardly necessary to explain to one with
such great knowledge as the Elchee, and to men of
such enlightened understandings as those by whom
he is surrounded, that Siyâvesh, son of Ky-Kâoos,
King of Persia, fled into Tartary, and took refuge
with Afrâsiâb, king of that country, who first gave

him his beautiful daughter Feringhees in marriage,
and then put him to death. The widow of the unfortunate prince was left, with her infant son, the
celebrated Ky-Khoosroo *, to the persecution of
her tyrannical father, whose conduct provoked the
vengeance of the king and nobles of Persia; but
you shall now hear the first battle, in which the
Persians were commanded by that hero Roostem,
and the Turks by their king Afrâsiâb."

After this prelude, Joozee Beg cleared his throat,
and began to recite in a voice which, though loud
and at times almost deafening, was not without
melody. The following is a literal translation of
the fight as given by our minstrel.

" Hearken to the sound of the drum from two
quarters; the restless warriors are impatient of
delay ; the trumpet's bray is heard afar ; and the
cymbals, clarions, and fifes of India and China join
in the clang of war ; the shout of battle reaches
the clouds, and the earth vibrates to the neighing
of steeds. When the noise of the approaching
army was heard upon the plain, the report was

---

* The celebrated Ky-Khoosroo of the Persians is the Cyrus of
the Greeks.

conveyed to Roostem, the avenger *. They told
him the force of Afrâsiâb was near; that his
great army rode over the plain as a proud ship
rides upon the seas; that his troops were in number like ants and locusts, and covered from the
eye of the beholder the mountains, plains, and
woods. When Roostem heard that the army of
the King of Turan † was in sight, he placed himself in the centre of his force; Zevâreh, his brother, was posted in the rear; Ferâmerz, his son,
was stationed in front; Toos, with his band, was
placed on the right. They were many in number,
but one in heart ‡. Feribooz, the son of Ky-
Kâoos §, was on the left, surrounded by a family
of valiant men; Gooderz covered the rear with his
relations, who were all free and independent ‖ heroes. The air was darkened with the swords of

* Roostem Keeneh-Kh'âh. The hero has this epithet as he was
desirous of avenging the death of Siyâvesh, murdered by Afrâsiâb.

† Tartary.

‡ " Their swords are a thousand, their bosoms are one."—Lo-
chiel's Warning.

§ Kâoos was at this time King of Iran or Persia.

‖ The term in the original is " Azâdigân," which means men free
or independent, that are not subject to the authority of others. heroes who went more with the cause than the leader.

the brave, when the glorious standard of Gâveh *
was unfurled.

" The leaders of the army of Turan now arrange
their shields. Bahamân commanded their right wing :
he was surrounded by men as powerful as they
were valiant. The left was led by Rahrem the renowned, and the centre by King Afrâsiâb in person.
The earth from the hoofs of the horses became of
the colour of an elephant, the air was spotted
with lances like the skin of the leopard. The
world had the appearance of a mountain of iron
with a crest of steel. The war-horses neighed,
and the standards fluttered, while the dark-edged
swords scattered heads upon the plain. Peelsem †
rushed from the centre of the army ; his heart was
filled with rage, and his visage covered with frowns.
He exclaimed aloud to the heroes of Iran, ' Where

---

* This famous standard was a blacksmith's apron set in jewels,
and was long the imperial standard of Persia. Gâveh was a blacksmith ; he overthrew the cruel tyrant Zohâk, and placed Feridoon
on the throne of Persia. When collecting followers, he carried
his apron as the standard of revolt against Zohâk. This apron remained the standard of the empire till taken by Saad-ben-wakâs,
who commanded the Mahomedan army that conquered Persia.

† The brother of Peerân-Weeseh, the favourite vizier and coun-
cillor of Afrâsiâb.

is Roostem? They tell me he is a dragon in the day of battle.' At this instant a shout was heard from Roostem, which shook all around. He said to his troops, ' Move not forward from the spot on which you now are. I go to silence this Peelsem, whose heart burns with rage, and whose visage is covered with frowns.' Roostem, foaming with passion, rushed to the front of the battle ; he couched his strong lance, fixed himself in his seat, and raising his shield to his head, he exclaimed, ' O Peelsem, thou celebrated warrior, hast thou called me forth that thou mightest consume me with thy breath ?' Thus saying, he struck his lance through Peelsem's body, and raised him on its point from his saddle, like a light ball. He continued his charge to the centre of the army of Turan, and casting the body from the point of his spear, exclaimed, ' Clothe this corpse of your friend in a pale * shroud, for the dark dust has soiled it.' Now the shout of heroes and the blows of maces are heard, and the voice of the trumpets shakes the earth. The deep drum sounds from

* The word means pale or yellow, and has an allusion to fear, of which that colour is the emblem in Persia.

the back of the elephant to the distance of many
miles * : the earth was wearied by the tread of
horses.   Each pool became like a sea with blood,
and each plain like a mountain from the slain, and
every stone was turned into coral.   Many were the
proud who were laid low on that day.   Heaven
seemed to call for blood, and the breast of a father
was devoid of mercy for his son.   From the dark
flights of the eagle-feathered arrows, with their
steely points, the air was deprived of the space
it occupied : the clashing of swords reached the
skies, and blood flowed from the boundary of
India to the Oxus.   The flashing of scimitars and
spears, seen through the thick clouds of dust, appeared like the forked lightning amid the dark
clouds of the firmament.   The day was made by
death, black, like the face of an Ethiopian.   The
numbers of the slain filled the roads, and the plains
were strewed with helmets and shields, and heads
were seen as if lamenting for each other.   The
hearts of the army of the King of Turan were
broken, and the field of battle became dark in their

* The word " meel" in Persian, is nearly our mile.

sight. ' Our good fortune,' exclaimed Afrâsiâb to his troops, ' is no longer awake, but sleepeth.' They left the field covered with iron, silver, and gold; with helmets, lances, and bucklers. The poorest in the army of Iran became that day a man of wealth, from the quantity of ornaments and jewels.

" ' Whosoever desireth to succeed, and to avoid trouble and danger, will not wander in the path of the wicked *.' "

Here our bard ended his battle, which differs in some stanzas from my copy of Firdousee; but that is not surprising, as I never knew two copies of this celebrated work that did not differ in a hundred places.

The attendants of the mission, particularly those who were of the ancient Persian tribes, and who hate the Tartars, were delighted with Joozee Beg's battle. We all expressed our satisfaction, and were assured by the minstrel that we were kader-dâns, judges of merit. But his delight appeared incomplete, until he heard the Elchee add to his thanks an order for a present of a few piastres. He then

* This last stanza is a reflection of the poet, referring to the injustice of the cause of the Tartars.

said he was "happy—he was honoured;" that he had often heard of the fame of the English nation, but was now, from personal observation, quite satisfied they were the first people upon earth.

The journey from Shiraz to Isfahan abounds with remains of the former glory of Persia. The greatest is the far-famed Persepolis of the Greeks, the Elemais of the Hebrews, and the Istakhar of the Persians. Every traveller has described these magnificent ruins, which the natives of the country distinguish by the name of Chehl-Menâr (forty* pillars), and Tekht-e-Jemsheed (throne of Jemsheed). Some conjecture that it was formerly a palace, others are quite positive it must have been a temple. I am much too wise to venture on speculations which have bewildered so many learned men. My reader must therefore be satisfied with a conversation I had upon this abstruse subject with some of my fellow-travellers, when I visited these monuments of ancient grandeur.

"This building," said Aga Meer, "was the house of Solomon, at least so I have read in the History

* Forty, both in India and Persia, is used to express an indefinite number or quantity.

of Shiraz." " And what did the foolish writer of
that book know about Solomon?" said Mahomed
Hoosein Khan; " but the author, I suppose, concluded, that because Solomon was the wisest of men,
he must choose Persia as his residence; and every
Persian will agree in such a conclusion." " No
doubt," said the mild Aga Meer, either not understanding the little nabob's sarcasm at the vanity of
his countrymen, or not wishing to enter into farther
discussion.

" People are divided," said the Khan, pleased
with his own sally, " whether this was a palace or
a temple; if it was built and inhabited by Jemsheed, it was probably both; for he says, in the
Shâh-námeh, ' By the divine favour, I am both a
sovereign and a priest *;' and if this first and most
wonderful man of Persia studied his ease and convenience half as much as his countrymen now do,
it is most probable, that, to save himself trouble,
he would join his palace and his temple together."

" You Europeans," continued Khan Sâhib, turning to me, " believe that Alexander, to please a

* Men-em gooft bâ-ferra-e-Eezidee Be-hem sheheryâree be-hem
Moobidee.

beautiful lady, set fire to this palace in a spirit of
mischief; we Mahomedans have the consolation to
think this proud abode of unbelievers was destroyed
when our first caliphs conquered Persia, through a
spirit of holiness. It was a rule," said he, smiling,
" of the first pious propagators of our religion, always to give to infidels an earnest in this world of
what they were to expect in the next; so they and
their profane works were included in one common
sentence of destruction."

Though neither the Indian Moonshee, Mahomed
Hoosein, nor the Persian Meerzâ, liked the levity
with which my little friend treated such a serious
subject; they saw he was in too lively a vein to expect to check him, but they looked grave. This
he observed, and to change the subject, asked me
what I thought was the meaning of a figure, to
which he pointed, half of whose body appeared
rising out of a circle, and to which wings were attached? I told him, he could not apply to one
who was more ignorant of such subjects than myself, but I would tell him what the learned of Europe had conjectured regarding this mystical figure.

The detail was long, and embraced a variety of

opinions; but I concluded by observing, that the figure was believed to be that of a Ferooher, or spirit, which, according to the doctrine of Zoroaster, is an associate of an existing being, with whose soul or spiritual part it is united before birth and after death.

" These Feroohers," said I, " were sometimes invoked as guardian angels: they were male and female, and were not, in their connexion with this earth, limited to human creatures; some of the race belonged to the vegetable world. Trees had their Feroohers." I was becoming more than learned, I was mystical, and on the point of showing some striking analogies between these aerial spirits of the ancient Persians, and the Sylphs, the Dryads, and the Hamadryads of the Greeks, when Khan Sâhib, anxious to make amends with his Mahomedan friends, for the slight which he saw they supposed he had put upon the first caliphs, interrupted me by saying—

" Well, God knows! however we may question the humanity, if not the policy, of extirpating whole races of men, because they did not believe exactly as we do, assuredly the founders of our holy religion have merit in putting an end to Feroohers, and all such trumpery as you have been talking about. There is enough of wicked flesh and blood in this world to give an honest man trouble and alarm, without his being scared in a wood, or frightened in his sleep by ghosts, spirits, and demons. The Glorious Volume*, thank Heaven, has put an end to all these gentry. But, after all, I really wish (looking round at the ruins) that while it conferred this benefit upon us, and gave us more space in the world, by the removal of some incorrigible infidels, it had spared some of their best works, if it were only as specimens of their folly and pride."

As he was concluding this sentence, Hajee Hoosein came from the Elchee with pipes and coffee for our refreshment. " You were speaking of good works," said the Hajee. " I was speaking of works," said the Khan. " It is all the same," replied the Hajee, determined not to lose an opportunity of showing his reading : " works are every thing in this world, as Sâdee says—' Alas, for him that's gone, and done no work ! The drum of departure has beat, and his burden is not made up †.'"

---

* Mes'hef-e-Mejeed, a pious allusion to the Koran.
† " Heif', ber ân kih reft oo kâr ne-sâkht
   Koos-e-rihlet zed oo bâr ne-sâkht !"

The admiration given to the expression and sentiment of the moralist of Persia did not prevent a
laugh at the manner in which it was applied. The
Hajee, however, was not displeased with our mirth ;
he was too full of Sâdee's apophthegms and stanzas,
and too eager to mix in conversation, to be particular as to the time or place in which he gave utter-
ance to his recollections ; and their want of application often rendered them more entertaining.

We returned to our tents with a resolution of
completing our knowledge of the wonders of this
place, by a visit to the famous rocks in the vicinity
of Persepolis, which are called " The Sculptures
of Roostem †."

Though there can be little doubt, from the similarity of these figures to those on the Sassanian
coins, that they have been made to perpetuate the
glory of the first sovereigns of that family ; yet,
when I on the ensuing day mentioned this conjecture
to my Persian friends, I found I was regarded as
an envious Frank, who wanted to detract from their
hero Roostem, with whose fame all that is valiant,
powerful, or wonderful in this country is associated ;

† Ncksha-e-Roostem.

and whose name has been given to this, as it has been to all other sculptures representing any warlike deeds, of which the precise history is unknown.

In order to make amends for the errors of my knowledge, I commenced a panegyric on. their favourite warrior. " We have," I said, " an account from the Greeks of a celebrated hero of theirs called Hercules, whom they have deified, and whom many of our learned confound with Roostem ; but this Hercules was, in my opinion, hardly fit to carry the slippers of your hero.

" The Greeks talk of the club of Hercules, but what was his club to the bull-headed mace with which Roostem destroyed whole armies ? Hercules, when an infant, crushed a couple of serpents ; but Roostem, when a child, brained a furious elephant : Hercules shot his enemy, Ephialtes, in one eye ; but Roostem did twice as much, for with a forked arrow he sealed in eternal darkness both eyes of the prince Esfendiâr : Hercules wore a lion's hide ; Roostem had, according to Firdousee, a vest made of the skins of several lions. Both heroes had supernatural aid, but Roostem seldom required it ; for he was endowed with the strength of one hun-

dred and twenty elephants *; and out of fifty thousand horses one only, the celebrated Reksh, was
found capable of bearing his weight.

" Hercules," I continued, " we are told by the
Greeks (who, however, are great romancers), accomplished twelve labours ; but what are these compared to the Heft Kh'ân, or Seven Stages of Roostem ? Besides, it is doubted whether Hercules could
ride—he certainly had no horse of any fame; whereas
Reksh excelled all horses as much as his rider did
all men."

This moderate and just tribute to the hero of
Persia quite restored me to the good graces of my
friends, who concurred with me in requesting our
old minstrel, who had charge of the horses of some
of our party, to recount to us the story of the Heft
Kh'ân, or Seven Stages of Roostem.   He could not,
he said, recite these great events as written in the
page of the immortal Firdousee ; but if we would
be satisfied, he could give us the tale in prose, as
he had heard it read from the Shemsheer-Khânee †.

* This, in the present *vapouring* age, would be called a hundred
and twenty elephant-power ; but I dare not take a liberty with my
text when recording facts.

† The Shemsheer-Khânee is a prose abridgement of the Shâh-Nâ-

Being assured that what he recollected of the story would be quite enough, and his audience having seated themselves beneath the sculptured rocks, he began as follows :

" Persia was at peace, and prosperous; but its king, Ky-Kâoos, could never remain at rest. A favourite singer gave him one day an animated account of the beauties of the neighbouring kingdom of Mazenderan * ; its ever blooming roses, its melodious nightingales, its verdant plains, its mountains shaded with lofty trees, and adorned to their summits with flowers which perfumed the air, its clear murmuring rivulets, and, above all, its lovely damsels and valiant warriors.

" All these were described to the sovereign in such glowing colours, that he quite lost his reason, and declared he should never be happy till his power extended over a country so favoured by nature.   It was in vain that his wisest ministers and most attached nobles dissuaded him from so hazardous an enterprise as that of invading a region, which had, besides other defenders, a number of

meh, into which are introduced some of the finest passages of Firdousee's poetry.
    * The ancient Hyrcania.

Deevs, or demons, who, acting under their renowned chief Deev-e-Seffeed, or the White Demon,
had hithcrto defeated all enemies."

" Is the Deev-e-Seffeed," said I, stopping the
narrator, and turning to Aga Meer, " believed by
modern Persians to have been a supernatural being,
as his name implies? or is this deemed a poetical
fiction of Firdousee to describe a formidable warrior, perhaps a more northern prince, and therefore
of a fairer complexion?" " Why," said the Meer,
" it is with us almost a crime to refuse belief to a
single line Firdousee has written; but though there
is no doubt he has given the account of these
Deevs as he found it, in the public records from
which he composed his great historical poem; we
find in some of our best dictionaries, such as the
Jehângheeree, and Boorhân-e-Kâtih, the word Deev
rendered 'a valiant warrior,' which shows that the
learned authors of these works entertained the same
notion as you do."

" If I had written a dictionary," said Mahomed
Hoosein Khan, " I should have solved the difficulty
by explaining, that Deev was a man who fought
like a devil."

This little sally finished our grave disquisition;
and Joozee Beg, who seemed not a little impatient
at the interruption, resumed his narration:

" Ky-Kâobs," as I said before, " would not listen
to his nobles, who in despair sent for old Zâl,
the father of Roostem, and prince of Seestan. Zâl
came and used all his efforts, but in vain; the
monarch was involved in clouds of pride, and closed
a discussion he had with Zâl, by exclaiming, ' The
Creator of the world is my friend; the chief of the
Deevs is my prey *.' This impious boasting satisfied
Zâl he could do no good; and he even refused to
become regent of Persia in the absence of Ky-Kâoos,
but promised to aid with his counsel.

" The king departed to anticipated conquest; but
the Prince of Mazenderán summoned his forces, and
above all the Deev-e-Seffeed and his band. They
came at his call: a great battle † ensued, in which

---

* " Jehân-âfireenendeh yâr-e-men est
    Ser-e-nereh deevân shikâr-e-men est."

† It was in this battle that the armies were, according to Firdousee,
enveloped in sudden darkness, as had been foretold by a magician.
The mention of this fact proves it to be the same action during which,
Herodotus tells us, a total eclipse of the sun took place, as had been
foretold by Thales the Milesian.—Vide Hist. of Persia, vol. i. p. 3.

the Persians were completely defeated. Ky-Kâoos was made prisoner and confined in a strong fortress under the guard of a hundred Deevs, commanded by Arjeng, who was instructed to ask the Persian monarch every morning how he liked the roses, nightingales, flowers, trees, verdant meadows, shady mountains, clear streams, beautiful damsels, and valiant warriors of Mazenderan?

" The news of this disaster soon spread over Persia, and notwithstanding the disgust of old Zâl at the headstrong folly of his monarch, he was deeply afflicted at the tale of his misfortune and disgrace. He sent for Roostem, to whom he said, ' Go, my son, and with thy single arm, and thy good horse Reksh, release our sovereign.' Roostem instantly obeyed. There were two roads, but he chose the nearest, though it was reported to be by far the most difficult and dangerous. Now," said Joozee Beg, " it would occupy the whole day if I was to relate at length the adventures of the heft khân: a short account of the obstacles which the hero overcame at each will suffice.

" Fatigued with his first day's journey, Roostem lay down to sleep, having turned Reksh loose to

graze in a neighbouring meadow, where he was attacked by a furious lion ; but this wonderful horse,
after a short contest, struck his antagonist to the
ground with a blow from his fore-hoof, and completed the victory by seizing the throat of the royal
animal with his teeth.   When Roostem awoke, he
was surprised and enraged.   He desired Reksh
never again to attempt, unaided, such an encounter.
' Hadst thou been slain,' asked he of the intelligent
brute, ' how should I have accomplished my enterprise ?'

    " At the second stage Roostem had nearly died
of thirst, but his prayers to the Almighty were
heard ; a fawn appeared, as if to be his guide, and
following it, he was conducted to a clear fountain,
where, after regaling on the flesh of a wild ass *,
which he had killed with his bow, he lay down to
sleep.   In the middle of the night a monstrous
serpent, seventy yards in length, came out of its
hiding-place, and made at the hero, who was awaked
by the neighing of Reksh ; but the serpent had
crept back to his hiding-place, and Roostem seeing
no danger, abused his faithful horse for disturbing

        * Goor.

his repose. Another attempt of the serpent was defeated in the same way; but as the monster had again concealed himself, Roostem lost all patience with Reksh, whom he threatened to put to death if he again awaked him by any such unseasonable noises. The faithful steed, fearing his master's rage, but strong in his attachment, instead of neighing when the serpent again made its appearance, sprung upon it, and commenced a furious contest. Roostem, hearing the noise, started up and joined in the combat. The serpent darted at him, but he avoided it, and, while his noble horse seized their enemy by the back, the hero cut off its head with his sword.

" When the serpent was slain, Roostem contemplated its enormous size with amazement, and, with that piety which always distinguished him, returned thanks to the Almighty for his miraculous escape.

" Next day, as Roostem sat by a fountain, he saw a beautiful damsel regaling herself with wine. He approached her, accepted her invitation to partake of the beverage, and clasped her in his arms as if she had been an angel. It happened, in the course of their conversation, that the Persian hero mentioned the name of the great God he adored. At the sound of that sacred word the fair features and shape of the female changed, and she became black, ugly, and deformed. The astonished Roostem seized her, and, after binding her hands, bid her declare who she was. ' I am a sorceress,' was the reply, ' and have been employed by the evil-spirit Aharman for thy destruction: but save my life, and I am powerful to do thee service.' ' I make no compact with the devil or his agents,' said the hero, and cut her in twain. He again poured forth his soul in thanksgiving to God for his deliverance.

" On his fourth stage Roostem lost his way. While wandering about he came to a clear rivulet, on the banks of which he lay down to take some repose, having first turned Reksh loose into a field of grain. A gardener who had charge of it came and awoke the hero, telling him, in an insolent tone, that he would soon suffer for his temerity, as the field in which his horse was feeding belonged to a pehloovân, or warrior, called Oulâd. Roostem, always irascible, but particularly so when disturbed

in his slumbers, jumped up, tore off the gardener's
ears, and gave him a blow with his fist that broke
his nose and teeth. ' Take these marks of my temper to your master,' he said, ' and tell him to come
here, and he shall have a similar welcome.'

" Oulâd, when informed of what had passed,
was excited to fury, and prepared to assail the
Persian hero, who, expecting him, had put on his
armour, and mounted Reksh. His appearance so
dismayed Oulâd, that he dared not venture on the
combat till he had summoned his adherents. They
all fell upon Roostem at once; but the base-born
caitiffs were scattered like chaff before the wind :
many were slain, others fled, among whom was
their chief. Him Roostem came up with at the
fifth stage, and having thrown his noose * over
him, took him prisoner. Oulâd, in order to save
his life, not only gave him full information of the
place where his sovereign was confined, and of the

* The kemend or noose of the ancient Persians appears to be the
lasso of the modern South Americans, and was employed to snare
prisoners as well as wild cattle. It is well known and often used in
India by some tribes of robbers and murderers of that country, who
cast it over the head of the unwary traveller with an expertness that
would do credit to a native of the Pampas.

Q 2

strength of the Deev-e-Seffeed, but offered to give
the hero every aid in the accomplishment of his
perilous enterprise. This offer was accepted, and
he proved a most useful auxiliary.

" On the sixth day they saw in the distance the
city of Mazenderan, near which the Deev-e-Seffeed
resided. Two chieftains, with numerous attendants, met them; and one had the audacity to ride
up to Roostem, and seize him by the belt. That
chief's fury at this insolence was unbounded; he
disdained, however, to use his arms against such an
enemy, but seizing the miscreant's head, wrenched
it from the body, and hurled it at his companions,
who fled in terror and dismay at this terrible proof
of the hero's prowess.

" Roostem proceeded, after this action, with his
guide to the castle where the king was confined.
The Deevs who guarded it were asleep, and Ky-
Kâoos was found in a solitary cell, chained to the
ground. He recognized Roostem, and bursting into
tears, pressed his deliverer to his bosom. Roostem
immediately began to knock off his chains: the
noise occasioned by this awoke the Deevs, whose
leader, Beedâr-Reng, advanced to seize Roostem;

but the appearance and threats of the latter so over-
awed him, that he consented to purchase his own
safety by the instant release of the Persian king and
all his followers.

" After this achievement Roostem proceeded to
the last and greatest of his labours, the attack of
the Deev-e-Seffeed.   Oulâd told him, that the
Deevs watched and feasted during the night, but
slept during the heat of the day, hating (according
to our narrator) the sun-beams.   Roostem, as he
advanced, saw an immense army drawn out : he
thought it better, before he attacked them, to re-
fresh himself by some repose.   Having laid himself
down, he soon fell into a sound sleep, and at day-
light he awoke quite refreshed.   As soon as the
sun became warm, he rushed into the camp.   The
heavy blows of his mace soon awoke the surprised
and slumbering guards of the Deev-e-Seffeed : they
collected in myriads, hoping to impede his progress ;
but all in vain.   The rout became general, and
none escaped but those who fled from the field of
battle.

" When this army was dispersed Roostem went
in search of the Deev-e Seffeed, who, ignorant of

the fate of his followers, slumbered in the recess
of a cavern, the entrance to which looked so dark
and gloomy, that the Persian hero hesitated whether
he should advance, but the noise of his approach
had roused his enemy, who came forth, clothed in
complete armour. His appearance was terrible; but
Roostem, recommending his soul to God, struck
a desperate blow, which separated the leg of the
Deev from his body. This," said Joozee Beg,
" would on common occasions have terminated the
contest, but far different was the result on the present.
Irritated to madness by the loss of a limb, the monster seized his enemy in his arms, and endeavoured
to throw him down. The struggle was for some
time doubtful; but Roostem, collecting all his
strength, by a wonderous effort dashed his foe to
the ground, and seizing him by one of the horns,
unsheathed his dagger, and stabbed him to the
heart *. The Deev-e-Seffeed instantly expired; and
Roostem, on looking round to the entrance of the
cavern, from whence the moment before he had
seen numberless Deevs issuing to the aid of their

* A representation of this combat is given in Dibdin's Decameron,
vol. iii. p. 475.

lord, perceived they were all dead. Oulâd, who stood at a prudent distance from the scene of combat, now advanced and informed the hero, that the lives of all the Deevs depended upon that of their chief: when he was slain, the spell which created and preserved this band was broken, and they all expired.

" Roostem," said our narrator, " found little difficulty, after these seven days of toil, of danger, and of glory, in compelling Mazenderan to submit to Persia. The king of the country was slain, and Oulâd was appointed its governor as a reward for his fidelity.

" It would weary you," said Joozee Beg, " were I to detail all the misfortunes and distresses into which Ky-Kâoos subsequently brought himself, by a pride and folly which were only equalled by the wisdom and valour of Zâl and his son Roostem; but one instance will suffice."

Hajee Hoosein, who was in attendance, whispered to me, " It is true, as Sâdee says, ' A wise man does not always know when to begin, but a fool never knows when to stop.' " I smiled, but shook my head, and Joozee proceeded.

" The event I am about to narrate," said he,
" appears so wonderful, that I should doubt its
truth, if I did not know it was written in the book
I before told you of.

" The success of his arms had raised Ky-Kâoos
to the very plenitude of power; not only men but
Deevs obeyed his mandates. The latter he employed in building palaces of crystal, emeralds, and
rubies, till at last they became quite tired of their
toil and abject condition. They sought therefore
to destroy him ; and to effect this they consulted
with the devil, who, to forward the object, instructed a Deev, called Dizjkheem, to go to Ky-
Kâoos, and raise in his mind a passion for astronomy,
and to promise him a nearer view of the celestial
bodies than had ever yet been enjoyed by mortal
eyes. The Deev fulfilled his commission with
such success, that the king became quite wild with
a desire to attain perfection in this sublime science.
The devil then instructed Dizjkheem to train some
young vultures to carry a throne upwards : this
was done by placing spears round the throne, on the
points of which pieces of flesh were fixed in view
of the vultures who were fastened at the bottom.

These voracious birds in their efforts to reach the
meat raised the throne—"

Joozee Beg here stopt, seeing me hardly able to
suppress a laugh. " You do not credit this story,"
he said. " You mistake," I replied ; " I am only
struck with a remarkable coincidence. In a sister
kingdom of England called Ireland, the natives,
according to a learned author, trick their horses
into a trot, by binding a wisp of hay to the end of
a pole to which they are harnessed, and, like your
vultures, they constantly strive but never attain
their desire: their efforts to reach the food fulfil the
object of the ingenious author of this useful inven-
tion. He was only a mortal, however, and could
do no more than impel a vehicle along the earth ;
the scheme of the devil is more sublime, and we
shall, I trust, hear of Ky-Kâoos reaching the seventh heaven !" " He was not so fortunate," said
Joozee Beg ; " for though he mounted rapidly for
some time, the vultures became exhausted, and
finding their efforts to reach the meat hopeless,
discontinued them ; this altered the direction and
equilibrium of the machine, and it tossed to and
fro. Ky-Kâoos would have been cast headlong

and killed had he not clung to it. The vultures
not being able to disengage themselves flew an
immense way, and at last landed the affrighted
monarch in one of the woods of China. Armies
marched in every direction to discover and release
the sovereign, who, it was believed, had again fallen
into the hands of Deevs. He was at last found,
and restored to his capital. Roostem, we are told,
upbraided his folly, saying

' Have you managed your affairs so well on earth
That you must needs try your hand in those of heaven * ?' "

Here the tale of wonder ceased, and a learned
dissertation commenced upon the genius and writings of Firdousee. It is only justice to this great
poet to observe, that the exuberance of his fertile
imagination, though it led him to amplify and adorn
his subject, never made him false to the task he had
undertaken—that of embodying in his great work
all that remained of the fabulous and historical traditions and writings of his country. We cannot
have a stronger proof of his adherence to this principle than his passing over, almost in silence, the

* " Too kâr-e-zemeen-râ nikoo sâkktee
Kih ber kâr-e-âsmân neez perdâkhtee."

four centuries which elapsed between the death of
Alexander the Great and the rise of Ardesheer or
Artaxerxes, the founder of the Sassanian dynasty.
Adverting to the history of the Parthian kings, he
observes, " When both their root and branches
ceased to flourish, their deeds remained unrecorded
by any experienced historian ; and nothing but their
names have I either heard or perused in the annals
of the kings of Persia."

I mentioned to my friends, as we were leaving
the ruins, the reflections which occurred to me on
these points, anticipating their approbation of the
justice I did Firdousee, but I was disappointed.
Mahomed Hoosein, the Indian Moonshee, alone
seemed to concur. " It is very just," was pronounced by him in an under tone. Meerzâ Aga
Meer said faintly, " Perhaps you are right." Khan
Sahib had a half-suppressed smile at the scrape he
saw I was in, from my qualified praise of the popular historian, as well as poet, of Persia ; while
almost all the natives of that country, and there
were many of the party, evidently considered my
criticism as bordering on want of faith in an author
whom they had almost worshipped from infancy.

I overheard Hajee Hoosein, to whom all the lesser persons in the mission listen as to an oracle, whisper to one of his friends, " Sâdee says, ' A wise man does not bring a candle to light the sun.' "

I left Persepolis with regret that my visit was so short; but the same ardent desire to examine this celebrated ruin was not felt by all our party. One of my companions, now no more, a gallant soldier and most devoted sportsman, was induced, by the game he found on the neighbouring plain, to delay his inspection of the palace of Jemsheed to the last day of our stay. On the morning we went to bid farewell to these remains of ancient grandeur, he promised to follow, but never came. When we interrogated him as to the cause, he answered with that simplicity which belonged to his manly character, " I could not help it: I was on the way, but found a fine duck in the stream that runs from the mountain ; it flew in a contrary direction, and I had to follow it several miles before I got a shot. There it is," said he, pointing to the bird which lay beside his gun, in a corner of the tent.

CHAPTER XIII.

TRAVELLERS AND ANTIQUARIES — WILD ASS — HAWKING — MADER-E-SULIMAN — AKLEED — MIRRORS — MEHDEE KHAN — ISFAHAN — PERSIAN CITIZENS AND PEASANTRY — SHAH ABBAS THE GREAT — HAROON-OOR-RASHEED — NETHENZ.

THE love of travel, visiting the remains of former grandeur, and of tracing the history of ancient nations, which is so common in Europe, causes wonder in the Asiatics, amongst whom there is little or no spirit of curiosity or speculation. Men who live in ill-governed and unquiet communities can spare no time for such objects from the active occupations incident to their place in society. In better regulated and more settled governments, the state, by divesting men of all immediate care respecting life and property, almost compels those of its subjects whose minds are active, and whose time is at their own disposal, to provide for themselves such a portion of vicissitude and trouble as shall overcome that apathy and inertness into which they might other-

wise fall.   From these motives they court toil and
care, and sometimes danger, to make them relish
the feast of existence.

Some gentlemen had accompanied the mission
whose chief object was to see Persepolis and other
remains of ancient splendour.   These motives were
unintelligible to the Persians.   The day we left the
ruins, Aga Meer, as we were riding together, expressed his surprise at men devoting their time to
such pursuits.   " What can be the use," said he,
" of travelling so far and running so many risks to
look at ruined houses and palaces, when they might
stay so comfortably at home ?"   I replied, with
some feeling of contempt for my friend's love of
quiet, " If the state of a man's circumstances, or
that of his country, does not find him work, he must
find it for himself, or go to sleep and be good for
nothing.   Antiquaries," I continued, " to whose
praiseworthy researches you allude, by directing,
through their labours and talents, our attention to
the great names and magnificent monuments of
former days, aid in improving the sentiments and
taste of a nation.   Besides, though no antiquary
myself, I must ever admire a study which carries

man beyond self. I love those elevating thoughts
that lead me to dwell with delight on the past, and
to look forward with happy anticipations to the
future. We are told by some that such feelings
are mere illusions, and the cold practical philoso-
pher may, on the ground of their inutility, desire
to remove them from men's minds, to make way
for his own machinery; but he could as soon argue
me out of my existence as take from me the internal
proof which such feelings convey, both as to my
origin and destination."

"There goes a Goor-kher" (wild ass), said
Mahomed Beg, the Jelloodâr *, who was riding
close behind; and away he galloped. Away I
galloped also, leaving unfinished one of the finest
speeches about the past and the future that was
ever commenced.

We pursued the Goor-kher several miles, when
we gave up the chase as hopeless. On our return,
however, we found plenty of other game; five hares
were killed by our dogs and three by hawks. When
at Shiraz, the Elchee had received a present of a

---

* Persian groom.

very fine Shâh-Bâz, or royal falcon.   Before going
out I had been amused at seeing Nutee Beg, our
head falconer, a man of great experience in his
department, put upon this bird a pair of leathers,
which he fitted to its thighs with as much care as
if he had been the tailor of a fashionable horseman.
I inquired the reason of so unusual a proceeding.
" You will learn that," said the consequential master of the hawks, " when you see our sport :" and
I was convinced, at the period he predicted, of the
old fellow's knowledge of his business.

The first hare seized by the falcon was very
strong, and the ground rough.   While the bird
kept the claws of one foot fastened in the back of
its prey, the other was dragged along the ground
till it had an opportunity to lay hold of a tuft of
grass, by which it was enabled to stop the course of
the hare, whose efforts to escape, I do think, would
have torn the hawk asunder, if it had not been provided with the leathern defences which have been
mentioned.

The next time the falcon was flown gave us a
proof of that extraordinary courage which its whole
appearance, and particularly its eye, denoted.   It

had stopt and quite disabled the second hare by
the first pounce, when two greyhounds, which had
been slipped by mistake, came up, and endeavoured
to seize it.   They were, however, repulsed by the
falcon, whose boldness and celerity in attacking the
dogs and securing its prey excited our admiration
and astonishment.

We had some excellent sport with smaller hawks
at partridges.   I was particularly pleased with one
bird which kept hovering over our heads till the
game was sprung, and then descending like a shot,
struck its prey to the ground.

We made three marches from Persepolis before
we came to any remarkable place; we then reached
some ruins called Mâder-e-Sûlimân, or the mother
of Solomon.   These have been almost as much
dwelt upon by travellers as those of Persepolis, and
conjectures are equally various.   Many insist that
this is the tomb of Bathsheba, the wife of Uriah,
the wife of David, and mother of Solomon.   To
this the only objection is, the belief or fact that
neither Solomon nor his mother were ever within a
thousand miles of this spot while living, and therefore it was unlikely to be chosen as the burial-place

of the latter when dead. Another account states it
to be the tomb of Sûlimân, the tenth caliph of the
race of Ali; but against this conclusion there is
decisive evidence in the very ancient style of the
architecture and the inscriptions, which are in the
arrow-headed character. Some antiquaries, puzzled
by these objections, have gone back to remote ages,
and determined it to be Pasargadæ, the resting-place
of Cyrus. I could only stay a few hours at this tomb,
otherwise this very important question might have
been decided.

The next place on our route meriting notice is the
village of Akleed, where the first mission halted for
some days. It is situated in a beautiful valley, surrounded by hills and watered by clear rivulets. The
gardens and groves in this town and its vicinity give
it an inviting appearance to a traveller in Persia,
which, with the exception of Mazenderan *, and
other provinces on the Caspian, may generally be
described as an arid country, without one great
river, and with few perennial streams †.

* The ancient Hyrcania.

† In Persia the term rood-khâneh, or, the bed of a stream, is the
common word for a river; an idiom which has probably arisen from
the fact stated.

If the report of the inhabitants of Akleed is to be believed, disease is almost unknown. A man upwards of eighty, who was praising the place to me, said, " We die of old age, but seldom from other causes. Then look round and see what a charming place it is. I have heard a Moollâh assert," he added, " that our town is called Akleed or Kaleed (the key), and, on account of its beauty and salubrity, is considered as a key to paradise."

" But you suffer from oppression, like others?" " Why," said he, " we are not exempt from troubles, but these come only now and then, whilst we always enjoy our pleasant habitations. We were in terrible alarm," he continued, " when we first heard of your approach: we were told that the Elchee was carrying a number of pier-glasses of immense* dimensions, as a present to the king; and that the inhabitants of the country, between Abusheher and Shiraz, were not only seized and compelled to carry these mirrors, but that all the principal men of the villages through which they had passed were to be sent to Teheran and punished, because some of them had been broken.

* Some of these mirrors exceeded eight feet in length.

" This you may suppose occasioned no small fright, particularly as we knew the Elchee's Mehmandar would take advantage of the pretext of carrying these presents to commit every species of extortion. You may therefore conceive our joy to hear that the Elchee, to save the inhabitants from such sufferings, had resolved to have the mirrors carried by mules. We were, however, not quite relieved from our fears till the whole passed through this place some days ago. Every mirror in its case was like a Tekht-e-Revân (or travelling litter), with shafts before and behind for the mules, by which it was carried. Then, besides twenty or thirty Ferrâshes to take care of these precious glasses, there was a party of horse to protect them; and the Elchee's head-carpenter, Randall Beg*, dressed like one of us, and with a fine beard, rode at the head of the cavalcade."

---

* Mr. Randall, who is here alluded to, was a very ingenious carpenter, who had been in an English man-of-war employed in discoveries. He had been in the habit of mixing with the natives of the places he visited, and was on this occasion of great use; for the Persian artizans, employed under his directions, worked with more zeal and readiness, from his dressing like them and living amongst them.

The story of the old chronicler of Akleed was perfectly correct; and what was more uncommon in a Persian narration, no way exaggerated. The Elchee, though he incurred considerable expense in providing for the carriage of these unwieldy but valuable articles, acquired more popularity, by the relief he gave to the poorer inhabitants on his route by this act, and by insisting on paying for the Soorsât, or provisions furnished to the mission, than by any others during his residence in Persia.

We passed several large camps of Eelyâts in our march between Persepolis and Isfahan. I had formerly seen enough of this race to satisfy me, that even the lowest of them were not only in a condition which freed them from want, but that they enjoyed a consideration in the community, or rather family, to which they belonged, that could not but contribute to their happiness. Their union and their bold character gives to this class of the population of Persia great security; and even when the tribe happens from political motives to be divided, which is often the case, the spirit of individuals remains unbroken; and if they are of a race which has reputation for courage and attachment, it is not unfrequent to see them in the service of those by

whom they have been subdued; nor do they in
such case conceal the hostile feelings they still cherish against their conquerors, who are usually indifferent to the sentiments they entertain or express,
while in their service, trusting for their fidelity to
certain ties and principles, which, as connected with
personal honour, are seldom violated by men of this
description.

These reflections forcibly recurred to my mind,
from a conversation I had, the day we left Akleed,
with an old soldier of the tribe of Mâaffee, who was
in the service of our Mehmandar.

" I have seen," said he to me, " nearly the whole
of the contest between the families of Zend and
Kajir.   I belong to a tribe firmly attached to the
former—I fought for them.   Our princes were
heroes in action, but they wanted judgment; besides, fortune deserted them, and favoured these
cruel Kajirs."   I looked round; and observing my
surprise, he instantly exclaimed, " What do I care
who knows my sentiments? Was ever man more
cruel than Aga Mahomed Khan! did not his wan-
ton atrocities exceed all belief! I will tell you one,"
he added, " that I myself witnessed.

" After the last and bravest of our princes, Lootf

Ali Khan, was betrayed and barbarously put to death; his Meerzâ, a respectable Syed of the family of the Prophet, was brought before Aga Mahomed. ' Why did you dare,' said the enraged monarch, ' to write me fermâns* ?' ' I did so,' said the Meerzâ, ' because the fear of Lootf Ali Khan, who was near me, was at the moment greater than of you, who were distant; but I trust to your clemency for pardon.' ' Cut off his hands and put out his eyes !' was the savage mandate, which was immediately obeyed.

" Next morning this Meerzâ's son was brought a prisoner to camp. He was sent for by the king, who addressing him, said, ' Go to your father; tell him the Prophet has reproached me for my injustice to him; I will do what I can to make amends: what does he want?' ' To go and pass the remainder of his life at the tomb of the holy Ali at Kerbela,' said the youth. ' Let him depart,' replied the king, ' as soon as his wounds will permit ; give him from me these three hundred tomans, and say, that horses, mules, and tents will

* Fermân means a command, and signifies here a letter or mandate addressed by a superior to an inferior.

be provided for his accommodation. Inform him,
I have repented of my inconsiderate violence, and
ask him to pray for me.'

" Now," said my friend, the Mâaffee, " many
think Aga Mahomed was sincere in his remorse;
but I believe he was only cunning. He saw that
every one was shocked at his horrible treatment of
a holy Syed, and he was anxious to regain their
good opinion. Nobody knew so well as that wily
fox how to manage men. But after all," he concluded, " bad as he was in other respects, he was
the soldier's friend, and so far better than his
nephew and successor."

" Assuredly," said I, " you cannot accuse the
present king of cruelty; he appears to me remarkable for his lenity." " What is the use of his lenity, if he neither gives his soldiers money himself,
nor allows them to take it from others? These
Kajirs," he continued, in no under tone, and with
fifty people within hearing, " are a sad set, and
we shall never have good times again while they
keep the throne."

Next day I spoke privately to this old soldier,
and told him I was afraid he might do himself in-

jury by the manner in which he had so openly
expressed himself. " Do not be alarmed," he said;
" there is now no prince of the Zend family in
Persia to compete for the crown. The Kajirs and
their adherents, therefore, take little heed of language that can do no harm ; besides, the king is,
as you say, a merciful man, and he has the good
sense to know he cannot alter the feelings of tribes
like ours. He knows, also, that however we may
talk, we shall prove true to those we serve, provided we are treated with confidence and consideration."

The first mission had halted at the village of
Taaghoon, within a short distance of Isfahan, where
we met a chief called Meerzâ Mehdee Khan, who
had served under Lord Clive in Bengal. He spoke
in raptures of that great man ; from whom, as well
as from General Carnac and others, he produced
testimonials highly honourable to his character.
He had retired, with the fortune he made in India,
to this, his native village. I was particularly
pleased with this old gentleman, and on our second
mission I inquired for him, but regretted to find
he had been dead two years. His son had succeeded to his property and situation as head of

Taaghoon, and appeared, from his conduct, to have inherited his father's sentiments of regard for the English.

Nothing can exceed, in beauty and fertility, the country in the vicinity of Isfahan, and the first appearance of that city is very imposing. All that is noble meets the eye: the groves, avenues, and spreading orchards, with which it abounds, concealing the ruins of this once famed capital. A nearer view, however, dispels the illusion; but still much remains of wealth, if not of splendour, and, were I so disposed, I might write a volume on its beautiful environs, its palaces, splendid even in decay, its college, with massy gates of silver, its magnificent bridges, its baths, its arched bazars, its fountains, its far-famed river Zindeh-rood, and the gardens on its banks, shaded with lofty sycamores, and filled with every flower and fruit of the temperate zone.

When the patience of the reader was exhausted by a minute description of all the beauties and bounties which art and nature have lavished on Isfahan, there would still remain to be described its two hundred thousand inhabitants, more than half of whom poured forth in their gayest attire to

the istikbâl, or meeting with the Elchee, the day
we entered this renowned city.

A few days after our arrival the governor gave
the Elchee an entertainment, which began, as usual,
with sweetmeats and fruit ; and after pipes, coffee,
tumbling, wrestling, and fireworks, a sumptuous
dinner was served up. Another day we were invited to breakfast with my old friend Hajee Ibrahim Kâledoonee, who gave us milk prepared in
seventy-two different ways, being, as Hajee Hoosein whispered me, in accordance with the seventy-
two sects in the religion of Mahomed. Whether
there was such a design or not I cannot say, but
the fare was admirable, and I was delighted to
find my friend, who is, besides being an extensive
farmer, a ketkhûdâ, or magistrate, of the ward of
Kâledoon in Isfahan, the same plain-dressed, plain-
spoken, humorous person we had left him ten
years before. He took us, as he had formerly
done, to the wonder of his quarter, the shaking
minarets *. When a person mounts to the top of
one of these, and moves his body, it vibrates, and

---

* The minarets of the Mahomedan mosques are, like the steeples
of our churches, of all sizes ; those we visited were of ordinary dimensions.

the vibration is imparted to the other, though at a
distance of about forty feet, the width of the mosque
to which they belong.

While my companions were trying this experi-
ment, and wondering at the cause, I remained on
the terrace conversing with Hajee Ibrahim   I noticed a small village about a mile distant which
seemed deserted. " Is that oppression ?" said I.
" No," said the Hajee, " worse." " Why," said
I, " the Tûrkûmâns cannot have carried their inroads so near the town." " They could not have
done the work so complete," said my friend, smiling. " Who has done it ?" I asked. " A doctor,"
replied he; " a proper fellow, who acquired great
reputation, and he deserved it, from the heirs of
his patients at least. That village literally pe-
rished under his hands in five years. Now he is
gone I know not where, but good luck attend him,
so he comes not again to our neighbourhood."

I went with some of our party to several of the
principal hemmâms or baths of Isfahan. That
of Khoosroo Aga I think one of the best I have
seen. When the first mission came to Persia,
doubts were entertained whether we could be per-
mitted this luxury. Fortunately for us the point

was deemed one, not merely connected with comfort, but with that respect which it was desirous we should receive from the natives of the country; and, viewing it in this light, the Elchee, by a well-timed liberality, converted impure infidels into favoured guests, who, instead of being excluded, were, at every town, solicited to honour with their presence the public baths.

The inhabitants of Isfahan are reputed quick and intelligent. They, like those of other large cities in Persia, differ much, both in appearance and character, from the peasantry who dwell in the villages. The latter, though I saw none in actual poverty, seemed from their appearance rarely to have any superabundance of even the necessaries of life. Though neither so well lodged, clothed, nor fed as the citizens of large towns, and perhaps occasionally subjected to more oppression, I always found, when I talked to them, that they preferred their actual condition; and though often loud and bold in their complaints of their superiors, they appear a cheerful and robust race *.

* I have been informed by one who had personal means of making the comparison, that he considered the general condition of the Per-

The food of the Eelyâts is derived principally
from their flocks, and they eat, with their cheese
and curds, hard black bread made from barley
and rye. The villagers in the cultivated plains
have less animal food, but more of wheaten bread,
fowls, eggs, vegetables, and fruits. Both these
classes are equally uninstructed; the wandering
tribes despise learning, and the inhabitants of ham-
lets and villages have seldom an opportunity of
acquiring it.

In the larger towns, and particularly those in
which there are manufactories, the case is very different; the inhabitants are generally well clothed,
and their whole appearance indicates that they live
in comfort. There are in all such towns numerous
schools, and in the principal ones colleges. At
Isfahan, almost every man above the very lowest
order can read and write, and artizans and shop-
keepers are often as familiar as those of the higher
ranks with the works of their favourite poets. The
love of such learning seems, in some of the youth
of this city, to degenerate into a disease. These

sian peasantry to be fully equal if not superior to that of the same
class in Russia or Poland.

Tâlib-ool-Ilm, or seekers of science, as the students are called, may be seen in crowds round the gates, or within the walls of its college, reciting stanzas, or discussing obscure dogmas or doctrines in their works on philosophy or religion, and they often become; from such habits, unfitted for every other pursuit in life.

The population of Isfahan, notwithstanding such exceptions, may be described as an active industrious people. They are considered the best manufacturers and the worst soldiers in Persia. But whatever may be their deportment in the field of battle, they are remarkable for the boldness of their language in the field of argument, and have great confidence in their ready wit and talent for repartee.

Some years ago, this city was governed by a brother of the celebrated Hajee Ibrahim, whose family at that time held several of the first offices in the kingdom ; and I heard that minister tell the Elchee the following anecdote :

A shopkeeper, he said, went to his brother to represent that he could not pay an impost. " You must pay it, like others," said the governor, or leave

the city." "Where can I go?" asked the man.
"To Shiraz or Cashan." "Your nephew rules the
one city, and your brother the other." "Go to the
king and complain, if you like." "Your brother
the Hajee is prime minister." "Then go to hell,"
said the enraged governor. "Hajee Merhoom,
the pious pilgrim, your father, is dead—" retorted
the undaunted Isfahânee. "My friend," said the
governor, bursting into a laugh, "I will pay the
impost myself, since you declare my family keeps
you from all redress, both in this world and the
next."

The merchants of Persia form a distinct class.
I had now seen those of Abusheher, Shiraz, and
Isfahan, and found their general character nearly
the same.

So long as they have no concern with state affairs,
and accept of no employment from government,
they enjoy considerable security. The plunder of a
merchant, without some pretext, would shake all confidence, and be fatal to that commerce from which
a great proportion of the public revenue is derived ;
the most tyrannical monarchs therefore have seldom
committed so impolitic an act of injustice. But this

class have suffered so severely in the late revolutions
of the country that they continue to act with great
caution. They are not only very circumspect in
their dealings, but, like wary diplomatists, every
merchant has a cipher, known only to himself and
his correspondents. By this means they receive
and convey that intelligence which is essential to
give safety to their speculations. Some few make
a display of their wealth; but in general their habits
are not merely frugal, but penurious. This disposition often increases with age to a degree that would
hardly be credited if we had not similar instances
in our own country.

The popular impression is so strong on this subject, that they relate the following story as a fact,
to exemplify it ·

A merchant who had lately died at Isfahan, and
left a large sum of money, was so great a niggard,
that for many years he denied himself and his
son, a young boy, every support, except a crust of
coarse bread. He was, however, one day tempted
by the description a friend gave of the flavour of
cheese to buy a small piece; but before he got
home he began to reproach himself with extrava-

gance, and instead of eating the cheese he put it
into a bottle, and contented himself, and obliged
his child to do the same, with rubbing the crust
against the bottle, enjoying the cheese in imagination.

One day that he returned home later than usual,
he found his son eating his crust, and rubbing it
against the door. " What are you about, you
fool?" was his exclamation. " It is dinner-time,
father; you have the key, so I could not open the
door ;—I was rubbing my bread against it, because
I could not get to the bottle." " Cannot you go
without cheese one day, you luxurious little rascal ?
you'll never be rich!" added the angry miser, as
he kicked the poor boy for not being able to deny
himself the ideal gratification.

Our stay at Isfahan was short. I regretted this
the less, as I had, on the former mission, full time
to trace those remains of the splendour of the Sef-
favean kings, which are still to be found at this
their favourite capital. The names of almost all
these monarchs are now forgotten, excepting that
of Shah Abbas the Great, who, in Persia, is not
only the builder of all bridges, cârâvânserâis, and

palaces, but his name is associated with all good sayings, liberal acts, and deeds of arms. I was really quite tired with hearing of this most gallant, most sage, most witty, and most munificent monarch, at his seat of glory; and when sixty miles to the northward of that city, we were entering the delightful little town of Nethenz, which lies in a narrow valley between two high mountains, I said to myself, " Well, we are now, thank God, clear of Abbas and his grand palaces; this scene of repose abounds in beauties for which he had no taste."

Hajee Hoosein, who was riding near me, said, as if he had read my thoughts, " This is a charming place, and the inhabitants are remarkable for their wit, as well as for their pears, peaches, and pretty ladies. When Abbas the Great—" I pulled up my horse, and looked at him with a countenance that indicated any thing but anxiety for his story; but not observing, or not choosing to observe, he continued :—" When Abbas the Great was hunting in this valley, he met, one morning as the day dawned, an uncommonly ugly man, at the sight of whom his horse started. Being nearly dismounted, and deeming it a bad omen, he called out in a rage to

s 2

have his head struck off.   The poor peasant whom they had seized, and were on the point of executing, prayed that he might be informed of his crime.— 'Your crime,' said the king, ' is your unlucky countenance, which is the first object I saw this morning, and which had nearly caused me to fall from my horse.' ' Alas !' said the man, ' by this reckoning, what term must I apply to your majesty's countenance, which was the first object my eyes met this morning, and which is to cause my death !'   The king smiled at the wit of the reply, ordered the man to be released, and gave him a present instead of taking off his head."

"Well," said I, when the Hajee had finished, " I am glad I have heard this story, for it proves your Abbas was, with all his fine qualities, a capricious and cruel tyrant." " No doubt he was," said my friend, " like other men in his condition, spoilt by the exercise of despotic power.   He had violent bursts of passion, but these were not frequent; and then he used to be very sorry for what he did when in one of his paroxysms ; and what more could be expected from a Shâhin-shâh, or king of kings ? There," said he, as we entered Nethenz,—" There

is an instance of the truth of what I say ; you see
that little dome on the summit of the hill which
overhangs the town. It is called Goombez-e-Bâz, or
the dome of the hawk. It happened one day that
this monarch, fatigued with hunting, had sat down
on the top of that hill with a favourite hawk on his
hand ; he called for some water, and a cup was
brought from a neighbouring spring ; the hawk
dashed the cup from the king's hand as he was
about to drink ; another was sent for, but the bird
managed to spill it likewise ; a third, and a fourth
shared the same fate. The monarch, in a rage,
killed the hawk. Before he had time to take another cup, one of his attendants noticed that the
water was discoloured. This gave rise to suspicions ;
and the spring was found to have been poisoned
with the venom of a snake or some plant. Shah
Abbas, inconsolable at his rashness in destroying
the bird which had saved his life, built this dome
to its memory, and is said to have often visited it."

After hearing this story, I was obliged, lest I
should have more anecdotes of this mighty monarch,
to confess that, though not a character exactly suited
to my notions, there must be some merit in a human

being who, in spite of his ordering a man to be slain
because he had an ugly face that frightened a horse,
and killing a hawk for spilling a cup of water, had
contrived to raise his country to such a pitch of
prosperity, that he was beloved, as well as feared,
when alive, and spoken of for centuries after his
decease as the author of all improvements.

The caliph Hâroon-oor-Rasheed occupies the
same place in the stories of the Arabians which
Shah Abbas does among the Persians; but the
" Arabian Nights" have made the English reader
familiar with the celebrated Commander of the
Faithful, which no similar work has done for the
sovereign of Persia.   The fame of the latter, even
in his native country, has not excluded Hâroon,
whom I have always found in works on the wisdom, moderation, and justice of monarchs, to occupy a very prominent place in Persian literature.

Aga Meer brought me one day a small tract,
containing an account of a visit of Hâroon to the
tomb of Noosheerwân, which was, he said, from
the lessons it conveyed, given to the youth of Persia
to study.   I perused it with pleasure ; and shall
give a translation of a part of its contents, as a

specimen both of the moral maxims of this country
and the mode in which a knowledge of them is
imparted.

" The caliph Hâroon-oor-Rasheed," says the author, " went to visit the tomb of the celebrated
Noosheerwân, the most famous of all the monarchs
who ever governed Persia.   Before the tomb was a
curtain of gold cloth, which, when Hâroon touched
it, fell to pieces.   The walls of the tomb were
covered with gold and jewels, whose splendour illu-
mined its darkness.   The body was placed in a
sitting posture on a throne enchased with jewels,
and had so much the appearance of life, that, on
the first impulse, the Commander of the Faithful
bent to the ground, and saluted the remains of the
just Noosheerwân.

" Though the face of the departed monarch was
like that of a living man, and the whole of the body
in a state of preservation, which showed the admirable skill of those who embalmed it ; yet when the
caliph touched the garments they mouldered into
dust.   Hâroon upon this took his own rich robes
and threw them over the corpse : he also hung up
a new curtain richer than that he had destroyed, and

perfumed the whole tomb with camphor, and other
sweet scents.

" It was remarked that no change was perceptible
in the body of Noosheerwân, except that the ears
had become white.   The whole scene affected the
caliph greatly ; he burst into tears, and repeated
from the Koran—' What I have seen is a warning
to those who have eyes.' He observed some writing
upon the throne, which he ordered the Moobids *,
who were learned in the Pehlevee language, to read
and explain.   They did so: it was as follows :

' This world remains not; the man who thinks least of it is the
wisest.

' Enjoy this world before thou becomest its prey.

' Bestow the same favour on those below thee, as thou desirest to
receive from those above thee.

' If thou shouldst conquer the whole world, death will at last
conquer thee.

' Be careful that thou art not the dupe of thine own fortune.

' Thou shalt be paid exactly for what thou hast done; no more,
no less.'

" The caliph observed a dark ruby-ring on the
finger of Noosheerwân, on which was written,

' Avoid cruelty, study good, and never be precipitate in action.

Moobid is the Persian term for a priest of the fire-worshippers.

' If thou shouldst live for a hundred years, never for one moment forget death.

' Value above all things the society of the wise.'

" Around the right arm of Noosheerwân was a clasp of gold, on which was engraved,

' On a certain year, on the 10th day of the month Erdebehisht *, a caliph of the race of Adean, professing the faith of Mahomed, accompanied by four good men, and one bad, shall visit my tomb.'

" Below this sentence were the names of the forefathers of the caliph. Another prophesy was added concerning Hâroon's pilgrimage to Noosheerwân's tomb.

' This prince will honour me, and do good unto me, though I have no claim upon him ; and he will clothe me in a new vest, and besprinkle my tomb with sweet-scented essences, and then depart unto his home. But the bad man who accompanies him shall act treacherously towards me. I pray that God may send one of my race to repay the great favours of the caliph, and to take vengeance on his unworthy companion. There is, under my throne, an inscription, which the caliph must read and contemplate. Its contents will remind him of me, and make him pardon my inability to give him more.'

" The caliph, on hearing this, put his hand under the throne, and found the inscription, which consisted of some lines, inscribed on a ruby as large

* The name of one of the months in the ancient Persian calendar.

as the palm of the hand. The Moobids read this also. It contained information where would be found concealed a treasure of gold and arms, with some caskets of rich jewels: under this was written,

' These I give to the caliph in return for the good he has done me; let him take them and be happy.'

" When Hâroon-oor-Rasheed was about to leave the tomb, Hoosein-ben-Sâhil his vizier said to him, ' O lord of the faithful, what is the use of all these precious gems which ornament the abode of the dead, and are of no benefit to the living? Allow me to take some of them.' The caliph replied with indignation; ' Such a wish is more worthy of a thief than of a great or wise man.' Hoosein was ashamed of his speech, and said to the servant who had been placed at the entrance of the tomb, ' Go thou and worship the holy shrine within.' The man went into the tomb; he was above a hundred years old, but he had never seen such a blaze of wealth. He felt inclined to plunder some of it, but was at first afraid: at last, summoning all his courage, he took a ring from the finger of Noosheerwân, and came away.

" Hâroon saw this man come out, and observing

him alarmed, he at once conjectured what he had been doing. Addressing those around him, he said, ' Do not you now see the extent of the knowledge of Noosheerwân? He prophesied that there should be one unworthy man with me; it is this fellow: what have you taken?' said he, in an angry tone. ' Nothing,' said the man. ' Search him,' said the caliph. It was done, and the ring of Noosheerwân was found. This the caliph immediately took, and entering the tomb, replaced it on the cold finger of the deceased monarch. When he returned, a terrible sound, like that of loud thunder, was heard.

Hâroon came down from the mountain on which the tomb stood, and ordered the road to be made inaccessible to future curiosity. He searched for, and found, in the place described, the gold, the arms, and the jewels, bequeathed to him by Noosheerwân, and sent them to Bagdad.

" Among the rich articles found was a golden crown, which had five sides, and was richly ornamented with precious stones. On every side a number of admirable lessons were written. The most remarkable were as follows.

First side.

' Give my regards to those who know themselves.

' Consider the end before you begin, and before you advance provide a retreat.

' Give not unnecessary pain to any man, but study the happiness of all.

' Ground not your dignity upon your power to hurt others.'

Second side.

' Take counsel before you commence any measure, and never trust its execution to the inexperienced.

' Sacrifice your property for your life, and your life for your religion.

' Spend your time in establishing a good name ; and if you desire fortune, learn contentment.'

Third side.

· Grieve not for that which is broken, stolen, burnt, or lost.

' Never give orders in another man's house ; and accustom yourself to eat your bread at your own table.

' Make not yourself the captive of women.'

Fourth side.

' Take not a wife from a bad family, and seat not thyself with those who have no shame.

' Keep thyself at a distance from those who are incorrigible in bad habits, and hold no intercourse with that man who is insensible to kindness.

' Covet not the goods of others.

' Be guarded with monarchs, for they are like fire, which blazeth but destroyeth.

' Be sensible to your own value; estimate justly the worth of others; and war not with those who are far above thee in fortune.'

Fifth side.

' Fear kings, women, and poets.

' Be envious of no man, and habituate not thyself to search after the faults of others.

' Make it a habit to be happy, and avoid being out of temper, or thy life will pass in misery.

' Respect and protect the females of thy family.

' Be not the slave of anger; and in thy contests always leave open the door of conciliation.

' Never let your expenses exceed your income.

' Plant a young tree, or you cannot expect to cut down an old one.

' Stretch your legs no farther than the size of your carpet.'

" The caliph Hâroon-oor-Rasheed was more pleased with the admirable maxims inscribed on this crown, than with all the treasures he had found. ' Write these precepts,' he exclaimed, ' in a book, that the faithful may eat of the fruit of wisdom.' When he returned to Bagdad, he related to his favourite vizier, Jaffier Bermekee, and his other chief officers, all that had passed; and the shade of Noosheerwân was propitiated by the disgrace of Hoosein-ben-Sâhil (who had recommended despoiling his tomb), and the exemplary punishment of the servant who had committed the sacrilegious act of taking the ring from the finger of the departed monarch."

Hâroon-oor-Rasheed, with all his fame for clemency, generosity, and justice, appears, from the very pages written to raise his fame, to have had, like Shah Abbas, his unlucky moments, when all his virtues were obscured by acts of violent and cruel injustice. Witness his putting to death the celebrated vizier, Jaffier Bermekee, and his vain efforts to rob the memory of that virtuous and great minister of his just fame.

Aga Meer related to me, after we had finished our translation, the following story, which I must add, though I hate dwelling long upon any of these eastern characters, however wonderful.

" Hâroon-oor-Rasheed," said the good Meerza, " when he had put to death the celebrated Jaffier Bermekee, not contented with this cruelty, wished to deprive him of those encomiums which the extraordinary virtues of that minister had merited; and he published an order making it death for any of the preachers or public speakers to mention the name of Jaffier. This did not deter an old Arab

from descanting with great eloquence on the virtues
of the deceased : he was warned of his danger, but
despised it ; and on being taken and carried to the
place of execution, all he asked was to see the caliph
for a few minutes. This was granted. The monarch asked him how he came to disregard his laws.
' Had I not praised Jaffier,' said the fearless Arab,
' I should have been a monster of ingratitude, and
unworthy the protection of any laws.' ' Why ?' said
the caliph. ' I came,' replied the Arab, ' poor and
friendless to Bagdad. I lodged in a ruin in the
skirts of the town, where Jaffier discovered me.
Pleased, as he afterwards told me, with my conversation, he paid me frequent visits. One night I
was seized and hurried away I knew not whither.
In the morning I found myself in a magnificent
Hemmâm, and, after bathing, was dressed by men
in fine robes, who called themselves my slaves. I
was then mounted on a horse with costly trappings,
and conducted to an elegant palace, where attendants, richly attired, welcomed me as their lord. Re-
covered from my astonishment, I asked what all
this meant. ' The habitation of a Fakeer *,' said

* Religious mendicant.

I, 'suits me better than this place; not a corner of
one of its saloons but is sufficient for my lodging;
besides, I could not remain happy, even in paradise,
if absent from my dear wife and children.' 'Your
lordship's family,' said one of the servants, 'are in
the inner apartments.' I was conveyed to them,
and found their adventures had been similar to
mine. They were surrounded by female slaves.

" ' While we were expressing our mutual astonishment, Jaffier was announced, and I found my old
visitor in the ruin, and Jaffier the vizier of the
great caliph, one and the same person. I endeavoured to make him change his resolution of raising
me to a rank for which I had no desire, and thought
my character unsuited: he was however inflexible.
'You conquered me in an argument,' said he, 'on
happiness being increased with the increased power
a virtuous man possesses of doing good. You shall
now have an opportunity of putting in practice all
those plans of beneficence to others which have
hitherto only employed your imagination.' I have
ever since,' said the Arab, 'lived in affluence; my
friendship with Jaffier only ended with his life; to
him I owe all I possess; and was it possible for me

to be deterred by death itself from doing justice to his memory ?'

" Though the caliph's pride was hurt, he could not withhold his esteem from a man of such courageous virtue. Instead of ordering him to be executed, he endeavoured to gain his admiration by more splendid generosity than Jaffier. ' Take that,' said he, giving him his sceptre, which was virgin-gold, studded with rich jewels. ' I take it,' said the grateful and undaunted Arab; ' but this, also, commander of the faithful, is from Bermekee.' "

Before quitting Nethenz I accompanied the Elchee in a ride through its streets and gardens, which are so intermingled as to give it a singular and pleasing appearance: you can scarcely tell whether you are in the town or the country. We saw plenty of the pears and peaches, for which my friend told me it was famous. As to its pretty ladies, they saw us, no doubt, through the trellis-work of their dark veils, while we could only dwell upon their beauties with the eyes of our imagination.

I complained to my friend, Khan Sahib, of the

privation of the innocent pleasure of gazing upon
the features of a lovely female; and then I added,
" What a mortification must it be for the lady to
have her charms denied that tribute of admiration
which is their due !" " True," answered my little
friend ; " it is very hard upon a few, but then think
how much numbers owe to that veil, which conceals
age and ugliness, as well as youth and beauty.   I
once," he observed, " fell violently in love with one
of these veiled ladies, whom I saw sometimes at a
window, and sometimes gliding, like a phantom,
through the streets.   She continued, for a month,
to occupy all my waking thoughts, and the image
of her beauties disturbed my rest.   I first cast
love-tokens into her windows, in the shape of nose-
gays; then I persuaded an old woman to pour out
all the raptures of my soul at the feet of the object
of my devotion.   To make a long story short, I
was at last promised an interview.   I waited with
impatience for the moment of anticipated delight.
When admitted into the presence of my fair I became wild with joy : I praised her shape, the sweet-
ness of her melodious voice, the captivating graces
of her manner, and, above all, her beautiful face.

She long resisted my entreaties to remove her veil.
This I deplored in the words of Hâfiz, exclaiming,

' O alas * ! O alas ! and O alas ! that such a moon should be
concealed behind a cloud.'

" What with prose, poetry, and flattery," added
Khan Sahib, " I succeeded at last. Would to God
I had not! but perhaps it has done me good ; for
what I saw of my imaginary angel has reconciled
me for life to veils and clouds."

As we were talking we arrived at a citadel which
was the residence of the old Hâkim, or governor
Hajee Abd-ool-Câsim, to whom the Elchee paid a
visit. We were received in a room at the top of
one of the highest turrets, from whence we had
a commanding view of the surrounding scenery.
Nothing could be more singular or beautiful. The
valley of Nethenz, which is inclosed by mountains,
is itself a succession of eminences and small hills.
The fruitful gardens, which occupied every spot
where there were no houses, extended eight miles.
Seldom above one, and never more than two of these

* Ei dereeghâ, ei dereeghâ, oo ci dereegh ! kih hem-choo mâh
pinhân shoodzeer-e-meegh !

gardens, were upon the same level : they either appeared in a circle, converging towards the common
centre of an eminence that rose above the others, or
were seen sloping in flights along the hills that bor-
dered upon the mountains. Rows of lofty sycamores and spreading walnuts marked the lines of
the streets and the divisions of the gardens; and
the latter were fenced round with thick mulberry
hedges, whose leaves, the Hâkim informed us,
fed innumerable silk-worms, the produce of which
formed the finest of the silk manufactured at the
cities of Cashan and Isfahan.

The sun was shining bright as we gazed upon
this enchanting scene, and its beauty was greatly
increased by numerous clear streams, which, pour-
ing from the neighbouring hills, either flowed or
were conducted among the gardens and orchards,
where they appeared lost, till seen glistening through
those parts where the foliage was lighter or wholly
removed.

The Elchee was quite delighted with the prospect.
After remaining for some time abstracted in contemplating its beauties, he turned round to the
governor, and with assumed gravity proposed to

change stations with him. " I should," said the
old Hajee, with a faint smile, " make a bad Elchee ;
and the pleasure you have enjoyed in looking at this
town from that window is the greatest you would
ever know if you were its Hâkim." When making
this last observation, he shook his head in a manner
too plainly indicating that the scene of abundance
with which he was surrounded was to him the source
of more trouble than enjoyment.

I mentioned my suspicions to my friend, Hajee
Hoosein, as he came to me with an evening kelliân. " Ah !" said he, imitating the exclamation
of his countrymen on entering the charming vale of
Desht-e-Arjun, " Irân hemeen-est ! Irân hemeen-
est ! This is Persia ! this is Persia ! But God is
just, as Sâdee says : he gives fertile fields, roses, and
nightingales, with wicked men, to one country, and
deserts and screech-owls, with righteous men, to
another ; and again he tells us, ' It is not the silk-
worm but he that wears the silk vest that is to be
envied.' "

I was quite satisfied with the meaning and moral
of my friend's quotations, though I confess I have
looked in vain over the pages of Sâdee to discover

them in his volumes.   But the Hajee, like many of his countrymen, has such a deference for that inimitable author that he ascribes all sentiments that appear just to him, as the sole source of human wisdom.

END OF VOL. I.

LONDON:
PRINTED BY THOMAS DAVISON, WHITEFRIARS.

For EU product safety concerns, contact us at Calle de José Abascal, 56–1°,
28003 Madrid, Spain or eugpsr@cambridge.org.

www.ingramcontent.com/pod-product-compliance
Ingram Content Group UK Ltd.
Pitfield, Milton Keynes, MK11 3LW, UK
UKHW010731190625
459647UK00030B/902